THE WELSH LEGAL TRIADS AND OTHER ESSAYS

CYMDEITHAS HANES CYFRAITH CYMRU

THE WELSH LEGAL HISTORY SOCIETY

Cyfrol XII : Volume XII

THE WELSH LEGAL TRIADS AND OTHER ESSAYS

Edited by

Thomas Glyn Watkin
Honorary Professor of Law
Bangor and Cardiff Universities

BANGOR
CYMDEITHAS HANES CYFRAITH CYMRU
THE WELSH LEGAL HISTORY SOCIETY
2012

Cyhoeddwyd gan
CYMDEITHAS HANES CYFRAITH CYMRU

Published by
THE WELSH LEGAL HISTORY SOCIETY

British Library Cataloguing in Publication Data. A catalogue record for this book is available from the British Library

ISBN 978-0-9926369-1-3

Printed in Wales by Infographics, Ltd., Cowbridge

Distributed by

Cymdeithas Hanes Cyfraith Cymru
Ysgol y Gyfraith, Prifysgol Bangor, Bangor, LL57 2DG.

The Welsh Legal History Society
Bangor Law School, Bangor University, Bangor, LL57 2DG.

CONTENTS

LIST OF CONTRIBUTORS

Dr. Rachael Jones is a schoolteacher, local historian and a Justice of the Peace

The Right Honourable the Lord Judge PC was Lord Chief Justice of England and Wales 2008–13, and President of the Selden Society 2009–15.

The Right Honourable the Lord Morris of Aberavon, KG, QC was Member of Parliament for Aberavon 1959–2001, Secretary of State for Wales 1974–79 and Attorney-General 1997–99.

Dr. Sara Elin Roberts is an historian specializing in *Cyfraith Hywel*, and the author of *The Legal Triads of Medieval Wales* (Cardiff, 2007; revised ed., 2011) which won the Selden Society's David Yale Prize in 2007.

Thomas Glyn Watkin is Literary Director of the Welsh Legal History Society and an honorary Professor of Law at Bangor and Cardiff Universities

ACKNOWLEDGEMENTS

The Contributors gratefully acknowledge the kind permission and courtesy of the following in allowing the texts of the lectures and the illustrations listed below to be reproduced in their respective contributions to this volume:

For ***The Welsh Legal Triads***

The Selden Society

For ***Welsh War Horses in Newtown : A Case from World War One***

The Powysland Museum, Welshpool	Figure 1
The Newtown Local History Group	Figure 2
The Ordnance Survey	Figure 3

For ***Dadleuon Dichellgar a Datganoli : Hanes yr Ymgyrch dros Awdurdodaeth Gymreig***

and

For ***Devious Debates and Devolution : The History of the Campaign for a Welsh Jurisdiction***

Sefydliad Materion Cymreig / The Institute of Welsh Affairs

PREFACE

THIS, the twelfth volume of the Welsh Legal History Society's publications, is published as the volume for the year 2012. It brings together a number of lectures given during or round about that year regarding various aspects of the legal history of Wales or the contribution to legal developments made by Welsh lawyers.

The volume takes its title from the first of the papers to be found in it, namely Dr. Sara Elin Roberts' 'The Welsh Legal Triads'. This paper is the text of Dr. Roberts' lecture to the Selden Society following its Annual General Meeting at the Old Hall, Lincoln's Inn, in July 2008. Dr. Roberts had been awarded the Selden Society's David Yale Prize earlier that year for her book, *The Legal Triads of Medieval Wales* (Cardiff, 2007), based upon her doctoral thesis at the University of Oxford and published by the University of Wales Press.[1] The text of the lecture has also been published by the Selden Society, and the Welsh Legal History Society wishes to thank the Selden Society and its officers for allowing the lecture to be published in this volume as well. The editor would particularly like to thank the Literary Director of the Selden Society, Dr. Neil Jones, for his co-operation in arranging the dual publication and sharing of the editorial preparation of the text.

The David Yale Prize is awarded for an outstanding contribution to the history of the law of England and Wales by a person under the age of 35. Awarded in alternate years, it was established in 1998 in honour of the Selden Society's then president, Mr. David Yale, QC, FBA, also a former literary director of the Selden Society. Mr. Yale is also a member of the Welsh Legal History Society and has been a loyal supporter of its work since its creation in 2000. It is a double pleasure, therefore, for the Society to publish the text of Dr. Roberts' lecture in this volume.

Indeed, it is a triple pleasure, as Dr. Roberts' lecture was chaired in July 2008 by the then President of the Selden Society, Lord Judge, the Lord Chief Justice of England and Wales. He also has been a member of the Society from its earliest days and very kindly agreed to the publication of his lecture, "The Welsh Language: Some Reflections on its History" in this volume. This is the text of the lecture which Lord Judge gave at Swansea

[1] A revised edition was published by the University of Wales Press in 2011.

University in June 2011 to inaugurate the Hywel Dda Institute, the Director of which, Professor R. Gwynedd Parry, chaired the event.

2011 was the year which saw the official status of the Welsh language in Wales being recognized by the National Assembly of Wales enacting the Welsh Language Measure. One of the challenges facing the use of Welsh for legal purposes is the revival of a legal register. The editor's lecture to the *Société Internationale pour l'Histoire des Droits de l'Antiquité* at Oxford in September 2012 entitled "Roman Law and Mediaeval Law in Wales" explored the significance of one rich vein of legal terminology in the native laws for determining the influence of Roman civil law on the native tradition.

In his evidence to the Peel Commission in the 1930s, an unsuccessful parliamentary candidate Ithel Davies said that "if the Welsh language is given its rightful and proper place in the administration of justice in Wales, there must be something like a fundamental reorganization of the judicial system in Wales to meet that measure of recognition". The question of whether the official status of Welsh as a language for the administration of justice and public administration in Wales together with the advent of both legislative and executive devolution require in some measure the creation of a Welsh jurisdiction was much discussed in 2012. Both the National Assembly and the Welsh Government instigated enquiries into the issue. The editor wishes to thank the Institute for Welsh Affairs for its invitation to deliver its annual Eisteddfod lecture on the topic and for its willingness to allow both the text of that lecture and an English version of it to appear in this volume.[2] The following year, he also addressed the British Legal History Conference at Glasgow on the meaning, or rather meanings, of the word *jurisdiction* in English, and how those meanings reflected the differing perspectives of the periods in which they were acquired. He begs the Society's indulgence for publishing several items of his own work in the volume, but hopes it will prove interesting to members.

---

[2] References to the two enquiries are given in footnotes to the lecture. Since the lecture was delivered, the Report of the Assembly's Constitutional and Legislative Affairs Committee has been published: see *Cynulliad Cenedlaethol Cymru: Y Pwyllgor Materion Cyfansoddiadol a Deddfwriaethol: Ymchwiliad i Awdurdodaeth ar wahân i Gymru* – Rhagfyr 2012 / *National Assembly for Wales: Constitutional and Legislative Affairs Committee: Inquiry into a Separate Welsh Jurisdiction* – December 2012.

The Society was fortunate in 2011 to have the former Secretary of State for Wales and Attorney-General, Lord Morris of Aberavon, as Youard lecturer. The lecture was delivered at Swansea University, and the Society is grateful to the University for its generous hosting and sponsoring of the event. Lord Morris' topic was "The Development by Attorney Generals of the Doctrine of Armed Intervention by States, without Security Council Authorisation to Avert an Overwhelming Humanitarian Catastrophe", and followed the publication of his autobiography, *Fifty Years in Politics and the Law*, by the University of Wales Press (Cardiff, 2011). The lecture throws valuable light on the importance of the rôle of the law officers in the development of the international law relating to the use of force.

Finally, war is also the background to Rachael Jones' contribution to this volume, "Welsh War Horses in Newtown: A Case from World War One". In it, she reconstructs – as in her contributions to previous volumes – the trial of a Newtown publican for failing to provision the military's horses appropriately. The paper illustrates further, this time from a legal perspective, the part played by horses in the Great War, an issue which has attracted much popular attention following the filming and spectacular stage production of Michael Morpurgo's novel, *Warhorse*.

As well as thanking the authors for their contributions, and the various societies and organizations mentioned above for permitting publication in this volume, the editor also once again wishes to thank the staff of Infographics Ltd., for their fine work in producing yet another high-quality volume for the Society.

Thomas Glyn Watkin
Cardiff
Gŵyl Ifan, 2015

THE WELSH LEGAL TRIADS

Dr. Sara Elin Roberts

IN this lecture, I will be discussing the Welsh legal triads, the topic of my 2007 monograph *The Legal Triads of Medieval Wales* (published by the University of Wales Press), which was awarded the Selden Society's David Yale Prize, although I will be giving a great deal of background before turning to the legal triads.[1] So, to begin, I will look at Welsh law in general, discussing what it was, the sources available today, and its significance. I will then briefly discuss medieval culture and education with particular reference to the lawyers and the use of triads. The third part of the lecture will deal with the legal triads specifically. And, indeed, that means that the lecture will be, perhaps appropriately, organised into one large triad.

THE LAW OF MEDIEVAL WALES

In his Hartwell Jones Memorial Lecture of the Honourable Society of Cymmrodorion in 1961, the historian T. Jones Pierce set out an imaginary scenario where Welsh law had continued to develop, and was recognised alongside English and Scots law in the House of Lords:

> ...the potentialities of Welsh law in the thirteenth century suggest that we could have ended with three systems of jurisprudence in these islands. In which case we might today have had a distinguished specialist in Welsh law sitting alongside his English and Scottish brethren (as Lord of appeal in ordinary) in the supreme court of the United Kingdom.[2]

---

[1] S.E. Roberts *The Legal Triads of Medieval Wales* (Cardiff, 2007). *The Legal Triads of Medieval Wales* was a re-working of my doctoral thesis, and presents these strange mnemonic sentences listing things in threes as an usable text for the first time. My threefold plan was to write a book that would be useful for those already working with Welsh medieval law, for Welsh historians more generally and for those looking at Welsh law for comparative purposes. I was honoured that the Selden Society deemed the book worthy of the David Yale Prize, and I was equally honoured to present the annual lecture of the Selden Society in 2008 to discuss my work on the triads.

[2] T. Jones Pierce, 'The Law of Wales – the Last Phase', in J.B. Smith ed., *Medieval Welsh Society: Selected Essays by T. Jones Pierce* (Cardiff, 1972), p. 379.

The scenario set out by Jones Pierce, whereby Welsh law might have formed a third 'system of jurisprudence' in the United Kingdom, would have been fantasy even by the end of the Tudor period, since the use of Welsh law in the courts in Wales was abolished with the Acts of Union 1536 and 1543. But up until then, Welsh law was in use in Wales, and it existed as a separate law, distinct from both English common law and canon law.

Welsh Law, or the Law of Hywel (*Cyfraith Hywel*), is attributed to King Hywel ap Cadell, or Hywel Dda (Hywel the Good) d. 949 or 950. It survives in around forty manuscripts, dating from the mid thirteenth century to the early fifteenth century.[3] Although the manuscripts are later in date, some parts of the law contained in them may be much earlier, but it is uncertain what link, if any, Hywel Dda had personally with the law. He may have had a role to play in developing some aspects of legal activity in Wales, possibly influenced by Athelstan in England, but there is no solid historical evidence to link King Hywel to the Welsh laws.[4] The prologues to the Welsh lawbooks give a story describing how Hywel gathered together the nobles and learned men, lay and ecclesiastical, to the White House (taken to be Whitland in modern-day Carmarthenshire) and together they discussed and brought the laws into order.[5] The prologues emphasise that the meeting was reforming existing law. This was probably an attempt to give the law a royal and ecclesiastical link, particularly as Welsh law was often under attack by the Norman clerics.[6]

THE TEXTS: WELSH LAW MANUSCRIPTS

The manuscripts are divided into four redactions or groups, and although each Welsh law manuscript is different and has unique attributes, the manuscripts within each redaction show similarities with each other in order and type.[7] The first three groups are named after eminent lawyers named in the prologues to each group: the Iorwerth redaction, after

[3] D. Jenkins, *The Law of Hywel Dda: Law Texts from Medieval Wales* (Llandysul, 1986), p. xxi.

[4] Jenkins, *The Law of Hywel Dda*, pp. xi–xvi.

[5] Ibid., p. xiii. See also p. 1 where there is an example of a prologue.

[6] H. Pryce, *Native Law and the Church in Medieval Wales* (Oxford, 1993), pp. 71–72.

[7] Jenkins, 'The Significance of the Law of Hywel', p. 74.

Iorwerth ap Madog; Cyfnerth, after Cyfnerth ap Morgeneu; Blegywryd after Blegywryd Athro. The fourth group is the Latin redaction of manuscripts written in that language.[8] I will briefly discuss the groups, although this is only intended as an introduction to another topic; the Welsh legal manuscripts are a topic in themselves which this lecture will not address in detail.

The Cyfnerth redaction has seven manuscripts. It is perhaps the loosest grouping of the three redactions, and is often seen to be the oldest redaction of the three as far as the content is concerned.[9]

The eight manuscripts in the Iorwerth redaction may reflect the law in Gwynedd during the reign of the two Llywelyns (Llywelyn ap Iorwerth, *c.*1194-1240, and Llywelyn ap Gruffudd, 1246-82), particularly Llywelyn ap Iorwerth, and the eight manuscripts form a close group. The Iorwerth manuscripts are also the oldest in date.[10]

The largest group is Blegywryd, consisting of thirteen manuscripts, fairly close in order and content, but further split into two groups. The Blegywryd texts are from south Wales. Several of the later manuscripts show signs of editing, and often contain additional material in the form of a 'tail', appended to the main Blegywryd text. This additional material was often taken from the other redactions, but some of it may be early, and it could also contain oral sources and legal rules in the forms of triads, some models of pleadings and material for training lawyers, and fifteenth-century Welsh laws.[11]

Finally, the Latin texts are usually treated together but there are five groups of the Latin texts. They were probably originally translations from some sort of Welsh legal text, and one of the manuscripts was then

---

8 A.W. Wade-Evans, *Welsh Medieval Law* (Oxford, 1909), pp. viii–ix; T.M. Charles-Edwards, *The Welsh Laws* (Cardiff, 1989), pp. 17–21.

9 Charles-Edwards, *The Welsh Laws*, pp. 20–21.

10 Jenkins, 'Significance of the Law of Hywel', p. 75; Charles-Edwards, *The Welsh Laws*, p. 38.

11 Charles-Edwards, *The Welsh Laws*, p. 20–21; C. James, 'Tradition and Innovation in some later Medieval Welsh lawbooks', (1993) 40 *Bulletin of the Board of Celtic Studies*, 152–154.

translated back into Welsh to form the Blegywryd texts. The Latin texts are not entirely in Latin, but are peppered with Welsh words.[12]

The law as found in the redactions and in the manuscripts can be separated into sections consisting of chapters or tractates. The order of the tractates varies in the manuscripts, and the tractates – and even material within the tractates – can be a mixture of early and late additions.

Although there are archaic elements in the lawbooks, the law was a sophisticated and highly developed system, with the lawbooks created by the lawyers for their own use. It was a compensation-based law.[13] In a hierarchical society, each person had a life value, *galanas*, which was to be paid to the family if the person were killed; it was calculated on a sliding scale according to status. A woman's value was calculated according to her husband's status, or for an unmarried woman, her father's. Women were not entitled to hold land or speak in court. Aliens, people from outside Wales, had very low status and few rights in medieval Welsh law. As well as the life-value, *galanas*, each person had *sarhaed*, an injury value, which was priced at half of a person's *galanas* and was an additional payment for a deliberate injury – the word *sarhaed* means insult. The word *galanas* can mean the act of homicide, or the payments for that act, and also a person's life value; in medieval Welsh poetry it is often used to refer to a disaster or lamentable death in general. Only in the case of accidental injuries and deaths would the injury or life value be paid without the *sarhaed* payment. Throughout Welsh law, the emphasis was on taking responsibility for actions, and this included vicarious liability: a father was responsible for the actions of his underage son, and the owner was responsible for any damage caused by his animals.

The *galanas* system of compensation for homicide was developed as a way of avoiding revenge killing and bloodfeud, as an extended compensation structure. In the event of a killing, the dead person's *galanas*, or life value, would need to be paid. Rather than the killer taking this fully upon himself, the obligation to pay was divided among his extended

---

[12] Jenkins, 'The Significance of the Law of Hywel', p. 74; H.D. Emanuel, 'The Book of Blegywryd and Ms. Rawlinson 821' in *Celtic Law Papers: Studies Presented to the International Commission for the History of Representative and Parliamentary Institutions*, D. Jenkins ed., (Brussels, 1973), pp. 163–64; H.D. Emanuel, *The Latin Texts of the Welsh Laws* (Cardiff, 1967), p. 53.

[13] Jenkins, *The Law of Hywel Dda*, pp. xxx–xxxi.

family, up to the third cousin, and payment was made in turn to the dead man's whole family, up to the same degree of relationship. The theory was that everyone in the killer's family would pay the price for a killing, and everyone in the victim's family would receive compensation. Although the rules for paying *galanas* are set out in the lawbooks, it is uncertain to what extent they were followed in practice.[14]

A fact about Welsh law which is often seen as surprising is that the death penalty was only used for certain cases of theft, and was not applied in cases of homicide. Theft was considered to be more serious than homicide in Welsh law as it was a stealthy act. As a stealthy act undermined society, certain cases of theft were punishable by death.[15] *Galanas* (in the sense of homicide, rather than the compensation payment which uses the same word), theft and arson were the three major crimes in Welsh law, and were called 'The Three Columns of Law'.

Other tractates in Welsh law include the laws of court, a long (and probably obsolete) section detailing the rights and the duties of the king and his royal household, the twenty-four officers serving the king, along with their rights and responsibilities, including their seating position in the court during a major feast, and payments due to and from them by virtue of their role. The laws of court are an idealized picture of life for the royal family rather than a discussion of courts of law.[16]

The laws of country concentrate on what could be called more practical law – the Three Columns of Law being the main part of the criminal law system – but also included in the laws of country were detailed laws on contract and suretyship, with the surety as a person to guarantee and enforce a contract or debts. Several sections discuss responsibility in communal agricultural situations: there are laws on corn damage, a section on joint-ploughing, and sections on injuries to animals. Land law is seen as a separate entity: the land law tractate sets out the details of how to conduct cases for lands, and how to claim land in law, and also lists the different

---

[14] R.R. Davies, 'The Survival of the Bloodfeud in Medieval Wales', (1969) 54 *History*, 343–357.

[15] Jenkins, *The Law of Hywel Dda*, p. xxx. Stealthy killings are only mentioned very briefly in the laws, but are very serious indeed.

[16] A full study of the laws of court can be found in T. Charles-Edwards, M.E. Owen and P. Russell eds, *The Welsh King and his Court* (Cardiff, 2000).

tenures in Welsh law.[17] The law of women has been much discussed, and it is an interesting section.[18] It sets out the status of women, and deals with marriage, divorce and children. There were several different unions recognised in Welsh law, varying from the casual and stealthy 'bush and brake' union to full legal marriage, and marriage changed in status after seven years. After this period, the couple could separate, and all of their goods would be divided, following the rules set out in the lawbooks, and excluding the land. If a couple separated with just cause before seven years were up, the woman received various payments set out at the beginning of the marriage – marriage was a contract, and both sides had certain obligations with payments or exchanges to make, one of the items changing hands being the woman herself.[19] Often seen as a sub-section of the law of women, the section on children covers paternity, how to claim or deny a child as one's own, and how to deal with offences by children (under the age of fifteen, their father or kindred would be responsible for them).

This brief overview of Welsh law demonstrates that it was separate from English law, and was a native Welsh system developed perhaps in an insular way, without too much borrowing from other traditions; although there are external influences, Welsh law was not derivative. Several of the concepts found in Welsh law are unique, and the Latin manuscripts leave certain terms in Welsh, possibly because they could not be translated. The most obvious of these terms is perhaps *galanas*, which is left in the original today – the word 'homicide' does not cover all aspects of the Welsh term and is therefore insufficient.[20] Often it was not the actual concept which would not translate, but certain nuances within one legal concept. In the medieval Welsh law of theft, distinction was made between stealing, which was taking something without the owner's knowledge or permission, and borrowing something without consent, which would not necessarily count

[17] Charles-Edwards, *The Welsh Laws*, p. 27.

[18] For a full study see D. Jenkins and M.E. Owen eds., *The Welsh Law of Women* (Cardiff, 1980).

[19] Jenkins, 'Significance of the Law of Hywel', p. 69.

[20] See Emanuel, *Latin Texts*, pp. 121–124, where several words in the Three Columns section, including the title, have been left in Welsh in the Latin text.

as theft.[21] In the Welsh laws, there was a term for taking without consent – *anghyfarch* – but even today, that idea cannot be expressed in a concise way in English law, and the cumbersome phrase 'taking without consent' is used in that situation with motor vehicles – for example, in cases of joyriding, where the verbal form of the closest modern English equivalent of the medieval Welsh *anghyfarch* is the rather ridiculous 'twocking', derived from the initial letters of the phrase 'taking without consent'.[22]

However, that is not to say that there were no influences whatsoever on the Welsh laws, nor similarities with other legal systems. Wales in the Middle Ages was not immune to external influences, and medieval Welsh law and early Irish law have a great deal in common.[23] Although Welsh and English law in the Middle Ages appear to be too different for overlapping and taking on legal rules from the other tradition with little adaptation, there is evidence that there was some borrowing, perhaps at a very early period. Several English loanwords can be found in the Welsh laws, but interestingly, they are mainly found in the laws of court, which were archaic and perhaps obsolete by the thirteenth century. The main loanwords are from Old English rather than Middle English – the Welsh *distain* is from *dish thegn*, one of the serving officers at the feast, and the king's heir apparent is called the *edling* in the Welsh lawtexts, from *aetheling*.[24]

THE MEDIEVAL WELSH LAWYERS

It has already been stated that the Welsh laws were composed with the lawyers as the intended audience, and in order to examine the role of the medieval Welsh lawyer, their texts are the main historical source. The

---

[21] Jenkins, following earlier authors, translated *anghyfarch* as 'surreption', which is the standard translation for *anghyfarch* in Welsh law; see Jenkins, *The Law of Hywel Dda*, p. 282.

[22] 'Twoc' is listed in the *Oxford English Dictionary* as a slang word, 'to steal (a car), esp. for the purpose of joy-riding'. Section 12 of the Theft Act 1968 discusses taking without consent.

[23] Jenkins, *The Law of Hywel Dda*, p. xxxiii.

[24] M. Lapidge, J. Blair, S. Keynes and D. Scragg (eds.),*The Blackwell Encyclopaedia of Anglo-Saxon England*, (Oxford, 1999), p. 444; R.C. Stacey, 'King, Queen and *Edling* in the Laws of Court', in Charles-Edwards, Owen, and Russell eds, *The Welsh King and His Court*, p. 47.

lawyers were a distinct group of high status men, similar to the poets; they were scholars with specific learning, some regulation of conduct and control of admission to perform the role. However, there is a clear distinction in the description of the lawyers in the lawtexts: the lawyers in north Wales were a different group to those in south Wales. The best lawyers were found in north Wales, in the kingdom of Gwynedd, and the northern redaction (Iorwerth) has different things to say about the lawyers to the southern redactions. In Gwynedd, the lawyers were skilled men, trained in their craft. They were men of high status – the highest in the country other than the king, with an exceptionally high life-value. In the royal court, the lawyer sat next to the king's son, and there was no death duty for a lawyer as legal knowledge was better or more valuable than anything earthly: there was no price on legal knowledge. However, there was a price on the lawyer's tongue, the symbol of his office: 110 heads of cattle, or over £10,000 today, more valuable than any non-royal person's life.[25] In south Wales, however, the lawyers were often local landowners with less formal training, and a less formal role; they would be less skilled and there would be more variety in what lawyers did and how they did it in south Wales.[26]

Different terms occur in the lawtexts for the lawyer, sometimes distinguishing the lawyer in north and south Wales. In Gwynedd, the Welsh term for the lawyer is *ynad* (*ygnad*), today translated as 'justice', and containing the early form 'gna', knowledge: the man with knowledge.[27] They were also called *brawdwr* (often in the south), meaning someone who is associated with *brawd*, judgments; and other terms are used, all dealing with justice and making judgments. Defining the actual role of the medieval Welsh lawyer is difficult, as the lawtexts are on the whole silent on court procedure – there are many references to the courts, but little detail as to how exactly they were held, where, or who did what. It seems that the definition of the lawyer in medieval Wales was looser than what we would understand today; the lawyer could perform the functions which would today be performed by a judge, solicitor, barrister, or legal secretary. They tended not to speak on behalf of a party in a case, as a representative –

---

[25] Jenkins, *Cyfraith Hywel*, (Llandysul, 1970), pp. 99–100.
[26] D. Jenkins, '*Bardd Teulu* and *Pencerdd*', in T. Charles-Edwards, M. Owen, and P. Russell eds., *The Welsh King and his Court* (Cardiff, 2000), p. 220.
[27] Jenkins, '*Bardd Teulu* and *Pencerdd*', pp. 220–221.

certain people required a representative as they were not entitled to speak personally in court, but the person who did speak would not be the lawyer. However, the lawyer advised the parties and sought to bring about a resolution to any dispute which arose. The resolution could be achieved through non-legal ways, with out-of-court arbitration, or in a more formal setting. The lawyer could prepare cases for people, without necessarily making the actual statements in court on their behalf. But it seems that the lawyer mainly acted as a judge, making judgments (which could then be challenged). So the term 'lawyer' in this lecture refers to someone expert in law, but who could carry out several different roles.

The medieval Welsh lawyer practised a specialist craft, and it was also seen to be a secret craft: there was a fine for any layman who eavesdropped on the lawyers' deliberations.[28] An ordinary man would find it hard to become a lawyer – the craft (like poetry, another mystical occupation) was normally passed from father to son. People banned from becoming lawyers included the king, anyone in holy orders, blind, deaf or mute men, lunatics, lepers, women or 'any layman without the right or training to become a lawyer'.[29] The last would seem to cover most people. In south Wales, the work of the judge was performed by the landowner by right, but in the north, it seems that the person with the right to be a lawyer would be one who had been fully trained.

Although little is known about the training of the lawyer in Wales, there is some relevant evidence in Ireland, and there is some evidence on the training in the associated craft, poetry, in Wales; there are also occasional references in the lawtexts themselves. The main point is that the lawyer's learning would be primarily oral, and he would need to know the law by memory, in detail. (This does not apply to south Wales where the landowners were permitted to use a book in court.) One short section in Blegywryd explains the training for a would-be lawyer, and it would have been a combination of learning specific sections of the laws, and observing other lawyers: a medieval pupillage.[30]

The specific sections that the lawyer would need to learn are found in the northern, Iorwerth texts under a heading: 'the justice's test book', and it

[28] S.J. Williams and J.E. Powell (eds.), *Llyfr Blegywryd* (Cardiff, 1942), 16.16–19.

[29] Williams and Powell (eds.), *Llyfr Blegywryd*, 102.28–103.14, 104.19–27.

[30] See Jenkins, *The Law of Hywel Dda*, p. 142.

seems that this would have to be committed to memory.[31] One important point is that the lawyers were not necessarily illiterate; several of the surviving manuscripts have signs of wear and tear, many are small and portable, and in the picture of the court justice in National Library of Wales MS. Peniarth 28, a Latin manuscript of Welsh law which has illustrations at relevant points of the text, he is seen holding a lawbook whilst making a judgment.[32]

A lawyer holding a lawbook whilst making judgment.
(National Library of Wales MS. Peniarth 28)

THE LEGAL TRIADS

Turning to the triads, a section of the Welsh laws which may be linked to the training and education of the medieval Welsh lawyers, the first and most obvious question about the triads is what exactly are they? The simple answer is that they are sentences listing things in threes. In the case of the legal triads, the three items are legal ideas or rules, grouped together under one heading. I refer to the legal triads, but triads are a common

---

[31] Jenkins, *The Law of Hywel Dda*, p. 141.

[32] D. Huws, *Peniarth 28: Darluniau o Lyfr Cyfraith Hywel Dda* (Aberystwyth, 1988).

phenomenon of Celtic literature, and not a specifically legal phenomenon – they are also not specifically Welsh, as there are large Irish collections of triads. The largest Irish triad collection is a mixed list, but the Welsh collections tend to be specific, and sorted by genre.[33]

One collection of non-legal triads was edited by Rachel Bromwich in 1961, *Trioedd Ynys Prydein*, ('The Triads of the Island of Britain').[34] These non-legal triads exist as a separate collection, known as an entity, and not bound with any other text; in contrast, the legal triads only exist within the law manuscripts. The non-legal triads are on various topics, but are all linked in that they discuss heroes, or important events, and were for the use of the poets or the storytellers: each item in each triad would refer to a separate story, so the triads are an *aide memoire* to the corpus of medieval tales, and there is evidence that they were actually used in this way – the earliest existing tales, the four branches of the Mabinogi, quote triads at relevant points. In most of the triads, though, the story is no longer known, so *Trioedd Ynys Prydein* is testament to the large corpus of traditional stories which are now lost.[35]

The triads were a mnemonic device, and would probably have been used as part of the education of 'learned' people in medieval Wales. Several elements of the poets' education are found in triadic form: the *Trioedd Cerdd* found in the bardic grammars point to the linguistic and composition skills they needed, and vary from being technical to giving moral guidance.[36] And, whilst this is true of the poets/storytellers, who we know actually did use the triads, the same can be said of the lawyers, who had a large corpus of legal triads: the lawyers in north Wales at least would have learnt the triads off by heart, and would refer to them in court, and they formed a part of their legal training.[37]

---

33 F. Kelly, 'Thinking in threes: the triad in early Irish literature', *Proceedings of the British Academy*, 125 (2003 lectures), pp. 1–18.

34 R. Bromwich ed., *Trioedd Ynys Prydein*, 2nd ed. (Cardiff, 1978), 3rd ed. (Cardiff, 2006).

35 Bromwich ed., *Trioedd Ynys Prydein*, 2nd ed., pp. lxxiii–lxxiv.

36 *Gramadegau'r Penceirddiaid*, G.J. Williams and E.J. Jones eds., (Cardiff, 1934), p. lxxxviii; and M.E. Owen, 'Trioedd hefut y6 yrei hynn', in J.E. Caerwyn Williams ed., *Ysgrifau Beirniadol* 14 (1988), pp. 91, 98.

37 F. Kelly, *A Guide to Early Irish Law*, (Dublin, 1998), pp. 253–8; D. Jenkins, 'A Family of Welsh Lawyers', in D. Jenkins (ed.), *Celtic Law Papers*, 125–-129; M.E.

Aristotle, in his treatise on memory, *De Memoria*, suggested using visual images as an aid to memory. He proposed that, by grouping ideas in threes, one could begin at a medial position when recalling them, making it easier to remember those on either side.[38] Since attempting to remember any items in a number greater than twelve is difficult, breaking up a large number of items to remember into groups of smaller numbers makes for easier recollection.[39] Three is considered to be a useful number for remembering – not too big, but not too small either; two and one are no good since remembering one item is easy and a pair is equally too few to be of use; five is difficult since it is an odd number and perhaps a little too big. Grouping in threes is still used as a handy device for learning things today. However, this attachment to the number three is not the only aspect of the medieval Welsh laws that shows numerical ordering. As well as groups of three, enneads, or nines, regularly appear (*naw affaith tan,* the nine abetments of arson; *naw tafodiog,* the nine tongued-ones; *naw cynyweddi teithïog*, the nine lawfully accepted unions), as do heptads (*seith escopty Dyfed*, an archaic section on the so-called seven bishop houses of Dyfed) and there are other examples of numerical grouping, for example, twenty-four officers of the court.[40] There is one example of a triad of tetrads (*tri phetwar yssyd*, there are three fours).[41] There are further links with the number three: an ennead may be significant because it is three sets of threes as in *Naw affaith galanas*, the nine abetments of homicide, where the punishments for the nine are organised in groups of three.[42] This may explain why there are so many enneads in medieval Welsh law. A pair of triads is attested, for example, *O whe fford y gwahan dyn a'e da*, in six

Owen, 'Gwŷr Dysg yr Oesoedd Canol a'u Dulliau Rhyddiaith', in J.E. Caerwyn Williams (ed.), *Ysgrifau Beirniadol*, 17 (Denbigh, 1990), 60–61.

[38] M. Carruthers, *The Book of Memory* (Cambridge, 1990), p. 63. Aristotle, in *De Memoria*, was referring to the technique of using individual visual or verbal associations. See R. Sorabji, *Aristotle on Memory* (London, 1972), p. 56.

[39] Carruthers, *The Book of Memory*, p. 107.

[40] *Llyfr Blegywryd*, 2, 30; *Welsh Medieval Law*, p. 2. Twenty-four is a number which occurs in other genres, the most significant instance being the twenty-four poetic metres. Heptads are also common in Irish literature, and there is a collection of them. *Corpus Iuris Hibernici*, ed. D.A. Binchy (Dublin, 1978), i. pp. 1–64.

[41] Roberts, *Legal Triads*, pp. 50–52.

[42] *Llyfr Blegywryd*, 30, *Welsh Medieval Law*, p. 37.

ways a man may be separated from his goods, which is again split into two groups.[43]

THE LEGAL TRIADS: THEIR PURPOSE, AND DEVELOPMENT

Trioedd Ynys Prydein, like the legal triad collections, probably began life as oral assemblages of triads. Rachel Bromwich points out that the triads in *Trioedd Ynys Prydein* were originally preserved orally, as they often occur in groups and contrasting pairs; the same may be said of the legal triads, and this lends further support to the theory that the triads were composed as mnemonics – that they were actually used orally for some time.[44] Testimony to the fact that triads started out as a simple mnemonic aid are the features which are found within each triad in order to make them easier to remember, such as alliteration and repetition.[45] Contrasting pairs occur in most of the triad collections, and legal examples include the long Cyfn triads on affiliating and denying a child.[46] A further development on this is having a list of triads on the same subject, or with a similar heading but different content: there are several sets of three triads, such as the triads on *rhwydi* (nets), and the *anhepgor* triads (concerning indispensables, that is, special things which the owners should not be without). There are also the five consecutive triads in Blegywryd, each starting *Tri lleidr...ysyd* ('There are three thieves…', with different classes of thieves listed).[47] These would have helped whoever was trying to recall the triads, but also contributed to the fixed order of the written triad collections – such triads were unlikely to be separated. As well as being purely legal mnemonics, legal triads also show that the redactors or composers were masters in the craft of writing: they show alliteration, compound words, and repetition or incremental repetition, a device often found in poetry and prose texts to emphasise a point or build up to a climax. These are all aids to remembering complex facts, but, at the same time, decorative devices. When the legal triads (or indeed any of the other triad collections) came to be written down, the

---

43 *Welsh Medieval Law*, p. 118.

44 Bromwich ed., *Trioedd Ynys Prydein*, 2nd ed., p. cviii; Owen, 'Trioedd hefut y6 yrei hynn', p. 90.

45 Roberts, *Legal Triads,* pp. 10–11.

46 Ibid., p. 10.

47 Ibid., pp. 108–111.

mnemonic aids were preserved but they also had a decorative function as well.[48] In Welsh poetry, the complicated metrical rhyme-and-alliteration system of *cynghanedd*, whilst decorative, may also be an aid to memory in a tradition which began as being largely oral.

Fergus Kelly notes that in the Irish collection, later additions often tend to have a 'punchline', or at least, a climax or anti-climax.[49] Although this is less commonly found in the legal triad collections – perhaps humour would not have been deemed appropriate in a learning environment or within the serious confines of law – there are occasional anti-climaxes, some of which are humorous.[50]

Whilst the triads started out as oral collections, they were written down. The main reason for this is probably that, as noted, in south Wales the lawyers were not the skilled, trained professionals as they were in north Wales, but local landowners who needed to be able to refer to the laws. Large collections of triads are included in the Blegywryd manuscripts, which are southern manuscripts (as well as Cyfnerth, also southern), but this is not the case with the northern Iorwerth manuscripts – the Iorwerth manuscripts do not include a large collection of legal triads, probably because the lawyers had no need of them. But once the triads became a written form, in the Cyfnerth, and more importantly, the Blegywryd manuscripts, there were some changes to the form, and indeed to the purpose of the triads.

Within the genre of triads, there are different types of triad. Probably the oldest type of triad in existence, given the original purpose of the triad form as a mnemonic, is the simple, short triad, with a 'heading' and three 'limbs' giving the three things, the three types of things, or the three ways of doing something.[51] Although useful as a mnemonic aid, these simple limbs do not, however, explain or expand on the rules contained in them. Therefore, a natural development is an extension to the triad. This can be done in two ways: the triad can be stated and the explanation can follow, or each limb can have an individual extension. There are fewer triads with long extensions in the earlier Cyfn collections, and many more of them in the later Blegywryd collections, which suggests that this was a later

[48] Ibid., pp. 10–11.
[49] Kelly, 'Thinking in Threes', pp. 10–12.
[50] Roberts, *Legal Triads*, p. 11.
[51] See ibid., pp. 7–10.

development. The fifteenth-century Blegywryd manuscripts contain examples of the most extreme form of extending triads, with the whole triad being a very detailed exposition of a particular legal point, lasting for three to four pages – these are far removed from simple mnemonics, if they are even capable of being committed to memory without great difficulty.[52]

I have already noted that there are collections of legal triads in the Welsh law manuscripts, but triads are not confined to the collections. Individual triads can be found at relevant points within a section of law, as a supplement or to summarize a paragraph of text. Also, several tractates in the lawbooks open with a triad, for example, *Arferion Cyfraith* and the *dirwy* (fines) section in Blegywryd, so the triad form had different uses: the original mnemonic purpose, with hundreds of those triads collected together in bulk, and also as a device for introducing sections of law.[53]

Another phenomenon found in the later manuscripts is the practice of having whole sections based around an individual triad. One Blegywryd manuscript includes a particular section, later in date – the Book of Cynyr ap Cadwgan – which uses a triad as a hook on which to hang some legal theory. The original triad is found in one early manuscript, and is as follows:

> *Tri grwndwal doethinab: mabawl ieuenctit y dyscu, a chof y gadw y dysc, a synhwyr oet y datcanu.*
> Three foundations of learning: adolescence and youth to learn, and a memory to preserve the learning, and the sense of age to declare [the learning].

Cynyr ap Cadwgan is a figure who occurs in the records in the early thirteenth century as the abbot of Llandinam in Arwystli (a cantref between Gwynedd and Powys, mid-Wales, on the Severn not far upstream from Newtown). He also appears as one of the *sapientes* in a land case in mid-Wales. He was a clerical jurist and his sons were declared official jurists in Arwystli by Llywelyn ap Gruffudd, prince of Gwynedd, in 1281.[54]

The book of Cynyr is a short book which, according to the explanation given in the manuscript, was compiled by Cynyr and passed down through

52 Ibid., pp. 7–10.

53 Roberts, *Legal Triads*, p. 9.

54 On the Book of Cynyr ap Cadwgan see Roberts, *Legal Triads*, pp. 9–10.

his family. It seems to be a handbook on how to learn, possibly how to learn to be a lawyer. The first line runs thus:

> *Ac yn gyntaf yd erchis vdynt dysgu tri grwndwal doethineb; sef yw y tri hynny….*
> First, I asked them to learn the three foundations of learning; those three are….

This is followed by lengthy sections explaining each item in the triad in detail. What we have in Cynyr ap Cadwgan's book is a study on a triad. The remainder of the book is also numerical and mnemonic: *Pymp clo yssyd ar ygneidaeth* ('There are five keys of justiceship'). There is evidence for other triads from the earlier, Cyfnerth, manuscripts being used as a basis for sections of law: for example, one triad is used as a basis for a section in the *Llyfr Cynghawsedd*, the book of model pleadings for the use of trainee lawyers. This demonstrates that the triads were known, and were used to form sections of texts by the fifteenth century. This is not a strictly legal idea: a literary parallel to this use of the triadic form as the basis of a text is Cyfranc Lludd a Llefelys, which is a story based on an extended triad.[55]

So, by the fifteenth century, the triads had developed and changed in purpose: no longer simple mnemonics for memorizing, they could be used as the basis for sections of legal writing, and were used as a starting point for developing legal theories. There is also further evidence that, by the time of the compilation of the legal triad collections, the triads were being used as more than simply a list of mnemonics.

Returning to a point made earlier, Welsh law tractates were not static and fixed, but were added to, and 'new' or additional material was appended to them, and often this material would be in the form of triads. Looking at the law of women in particular, as a case study, the women tractate within the lawtexts does not seem to show very much development, and could be called old-fashioned in its attitude towards women: the tractate is paternalistic, giving women very few rights and women were more or less seen as part of a man's property.[56] This is at odds with what was happening

---

[55] Ibid., p. 10.

[56] This case study is presented in S.E. Roberts, 'Emerging from the Bushes: the Welsh Law of Women in the Legal Triads', in J.F. Eska ed., *Law, Literature and Society: CSANA Yearbook 7* (Dublin, 2008), pp. 58–76.

in a social context, however. Attitudes towards women and their rights were changing in thirteenth-century Wales, but the changes are not reflected in the women tractate in Welsh law. The text was not rewritten to reflect the attitudes of the time, and does not reflect changes happening in Welsh law. There were changes to the law of women, but the changes occurred outside the tractate, and some of the development is found in the legal triads. The triads focusing on women found in the legal triad collections in Blegywryd show a great deal of development.

We see the idea of women as practically chattels in the women tractate being re-thought, and the feelings of women being taken into consideration – for an assault on the body, a woman would receive compensation personally according to one triad, as she herself would have been injured, rather than have the compensation go directly to her husband.[57] Some material is re-worked in the triads, reflecting a more sensitive attitude towards women. One of the triads gives a new section of law, or at least a material not contained within the women tractate or elsewhere in the law manuscripts – the law of *twyllforwyn*, a false virgin, is labelled as a tractate, *A hynny yw kyfreith twylluorwyn*.[58] Labelling in this way was often used authoritatively for tractates, and the wording is definitive: it is referring to a particular legal rule. The interesting point is that this material, a specific section of law, was not added or incorporated into the main tractate on the law of women, but was included in a triad. The triad may even have been constructed especially to include this material: there was a section of law to be introduced, and two other items were grouped with the *twyllforwyn* material in order to create the triad. The first two items in the triad are very short, compared to the third item.[59] There is evidence elsewhere in the triad collections for this type of composition: occasionally, one item in a triad hangs loosely or fits badly with the other two.

A fuller study of the triads on women in the triad collection also supports this – it demonstrates that triads were seen as an appropriate way of including legal thinking in the lawtexts, either new developments, or sections of law not included elsewhere. There was refinement and adjustment to Welsh law, and the lawyers were constantly working on this; this is why it is difficult to date Welsh law as a whole. The important point

[57] Roberts, 'Emerging from the Bushes', pp. 66–67.
[58] Ibid., pp. 70–72.
[59] Ibid., pp. 70–72.

is that the development could be summarized in the triad. Dafydd Jenkins states that part of what makes Welsh law valuable is the evidence for how the lawyers applied the principles of the law to meet new situations. Originally, the triads were part of what the medieval Welsh lawyer had to learn. However, dismissing the triad collections as only mnemonics, or calling them merely literary forms would be oversimplification. They are – or were – mnemonics and a literary form, but it appears that the triads served a greater purpose in the mind of the Welsh lawyer, and the triad collections can be studies in their own right, as a melting pot for medieval Welsh legal thinking and further development of already sophisticated medieval Welsh law.[60]

After 1536, only one or two cases were heard using Welsh law, and the use of Welsh law effectively came to an end. Jones Pierce's imaginary vision of the three laws of Britain together in the House of Lords was most definitely his own imagination, and no part of Welsh law was ever knowingly incorporated into modern English law. (The fact that some aspects of Welsh law might be useful in English law today is a topic for another discussion!) Sections of Welsh law were archaic and not observed even in the Middle Ages, so Jones Pierce's grandiose claim would have been unlikely to have been substantiated. However, some of the concepts of Welsh law were basic and general, and some survive informally, in market places or folk memory. The influence of medieval Welsh law in England before 1536 was minimal, but in Wales it was crucial: the lawbooks were far more than legal documents. They are a large part of the surviving Welsh language manuscripts from the Middle Ages, and are significant prose texts, full of technical and everyday medieval Welsh vocabulary. The law gave the Welsh language, to some extent, a dignity, and several of the legal terms are part of the native vocabulary rather than being English or Latin borrowings; the Welsh laws may also have contributed to the survival of the Welsh language,[61] and was a great unifier for the 'politically fragmented' Welsh people during the Middle Ages, as the one native institution which applied to every Welshman.[62]

---

60 Ibid., pp. 75–76.

61 Emanuel, *Latin Texts*, p. xxxvi.

62 Emanuel, *Latin Texts*, p. xxvi.

APPENDIX

ILLUSTRATIVE EXAMPLES OF TRIADS

1. Alliteration:

Tri gwanas gwayw.
Three thrusts of a spear.

Tri enw rhingyll y sydd: 'gwaedd gwlad', a 'garw gychwedl gwas y cynghellor', a 'rhingyll'.

There are three names for the *rhingyll*: 'the shriek of the country', and 'bad news the servant of the *cynghellor*', and '*rhingyll*'.

2. Repetition:

Tair cyflafan os gwna dyn yn ei wlad y dyly ei fab colli tref ei dad o'e hachos o gyfraith: lladd ei arglwydd, a lladd y pencenedl, a lladd y teispantyle, rhag trymed y cyflafanau hynny.

Three offences for which, if a man commits them in his own country, his son should lose his patrimony by law: killing his lord, and killing his head of kindred, and killing his representative, because of the seriousness of those offences.

Tri ofer llaeth y sydd: llaeth caseg, a llaeth gast, a llaeth cath, can ni diwygir un ohonynt.

There are three useless milks: the milk of a mare, and the milk of a bitch, and the milk of a cat.

3. Contrasting pairs:

Tri mab rhydd o gaeth: ysgolhaig, a bardd, a gof. Tri mab caeth o rydd: eu meibion hwynt hwy.

Three free sons from slave [fathers]: a cleric, a poet, and a blacksmith. Three slave sons from free [fathers]: their sons.

4. Lists on the same subject:

Tri lleidr camlyrus y sydd…
There are three thieves liable to *camlwrw* [serious fine] …

Tri lleidr dirwyus y sydd…
There are three thieves liable to *dirwy* [lesser fine]…

Tri lleidr gwerth y sydd…
There are three thieves liable to be sold…

Tri lleidr crogadwy y sydd…
There are three thieves liable to be hanged…

Tri lleidr a ddiainc o ledrad cyfaddef…
Three thieves who escape despite an acknowledged theft…

5. Humour:

Tri pheth ni thelir kyn coller yn ranty: kyllell, a chledyf, a llawdyr.

Three things which are not paid for if they are lost in a house where someone is lodged: a knife, and a sword, and trousers.

THE TRIAD GENRE

1. Simple triad:

Teir gormes doeth ynt: meddawt, a dryc annyan, a godinheb.

These are the three oppressors of the wise: drunkenness, and bad temper, and adultery.

2. Extensions:

Tri phryf a dyly brenhin ev gwerth pa le bynnac y llader: [1.] *llostlydan,* [2.] *a beleu,* [3.] *a charlwng*; [Extension] *canys ohonunt wy y dylyur wneuthur amarwyeu y dillad y brenhin.*

Three animals to whose value the king is entitled wherever they are killed: a beaver, and a sable, and a stoat; because from them the borders of the king's clothes should be made.

Tri gwerth kyfureith beichyogi gwreic: [1.] *gwaed kyn delwad,* [Extension] *wyth a deugein a dal o chollir drwy greulonder.* [2.] *Eil yw kyn dyuod eneid yndaw,* [Extension] *trayan yr alanas a dal.* [3.] *Y trydyd yw gwedy el eneid yndaw,* [Extension] *galanas gwbyl a delir amdanaw o chollir trwy grevlonder.*

Three legal values of a woman's foetus: blood before formation, it is worth forty-eight [pence] if it is lost through cruelty. The second is before life enters it, a third of the *galanas* is paid for it. The third is after life enters it its full *galanas* ought to be paid if it is lost through cruelty.

3. Developing Welsh law

Teir sarhaet gwreic ynt, vn a drycheif, ac vn a ostwg, ac vn ysyd sarhaet gwbyl: kyntaf yw bot genthi o'e hanuod, a honno gan vn drychafel y telir idi. Yr eil yw rodi cussan idi o'e hanuod, a honno a ostwg, y trayan a vyd eisseu idi. Trydyd yw y phaluu o'e hanuod, a honno yssyd sarhaet gwbyl idi; ac os gwryawc vyd, herwyd breint y gwr y telir idi.

These are the three *sarhaeds* of a woman, one which is augmented, one which is decreased, and one which is complete *sarhaed*: the first is to have intercourse with her against her will, and that is paid to her with one augmentation. The second is to give her a kiss against her will, and that is decreased, a third is lacking from it. The third is to grope her against her will, and that is complete *sarhaed* to her; and if she is married, it is paid to her according to the status of her husband.

Tri hwrd ny diwygir: vn yw hwrd gwr ac aryf yn y elyn am y gar gwedy ys gofynho yn tri dadleu, a heb gaffel iawn; kyt as llado, nys diwc. Eil yw hwrd gwreic wryawc yn y chywyres a'e dwy law yn y kyfarffont; kyt bo marw, ny diwygir. Trydyd yw o rodir twylluorwyn y wr, a gwedy y phroui y chaffel yn twylluorwyn, a mach ar y morwyndawt; kyt as gwanho a'e law neu a'e troet dros y gwely ac nas llado, nys diwc. Yr hwrd heuyt a wanho a bonllost yndi ny diwygir idi; llather y chrys, hagen, yn gyfuwch a thal y phedrein, a'r tu racdi yn gyfuwch a gwarr y chont, a'e gellwg a'r hwrd hwnnw yndi heb y diuwyn idi. A hynny yw kyfreith twylluorwyn.

Three thrusts for which reparation is not made: one is the thrust of a man with a weapon into his enemy [in revenge] for his relative after he has asked [for redress] in three sessions, without receiving redress; although he may kill him, he does not pay compensation. The second is a thrust of a married woman at her [husband's] concubine with her two hands when they meet; although she may die, compensation is not paid. The third is if a false virgin is given to a man, and after testing her she is found to be a false virgin, with surety on her virginity; although he shoves her with his hand or his foot over the bed and does not kill her, he does not pay compensation. Also there is no redress to her for the thrust he made into her with his penis; however, let her shift be cut as high as the top of her buttocks, and in front as high as the top of her cunt, and she is released with that thrust in her without compensating her for it. And that is the law of a false virgin.

ROMAN LAW AND MEDIAEVAL LAW IN WALES[1]

Thomas Glyn Watkin

THE appointment of Alberico Gentili as Regius Professor of Civil Law in Oxford in 1587 marked an important moment in the history of that chair's development, for it was the first occasion since its establishment by King Henry VIII in 1540 that the holder of the chair would be a distinguished civilian legal scholar from mainland Europe. Gentili found himself in England more or less as a consequence of the Reformation, for his father had embraced Protestantism and, as a consequence, had left his native Italy. Gentili thus came to Oxford's chair of civil law as a kind of refugee, enriching the legal scholarship of the age in this country in much the same manner as in a later century, legal scholarship in Oxford would once again be enriched by an influx of academics seeking a safe haven from persecution on the grounds of their religious faith.[2]

Gentili however was not the first 'foreigner' to hold the chair, for very few of his predecessors had been English. Of the seven previous incumbents since the chair's inception in 1540, the majority had come from outside of England, although not so far away as Italy. William Aubrey, professor from 1553 until 1559, John Griffith who succeeded him and held the chair until 1566, his successor Robert Lougher who was professor until 1577 and Griffith Lloyd who held the chair until 1586, all came from Wales. This is all the more remarkable given that the incorporation of Wales into the dominions of the English king had only occurred a generation earlier, albeit that the Tudor dynasty had acknowledged roots in Wales. The eminent Welsh civilians who aspired to the Regius chair were by no means the only distinguished civil and canon lawyers to hail from Wales at this time. Indeed, roughly a third of all the advocates admitted to practise before the ecclesiastical courts and the Admiral's court in London during the sixteenth century – the courts which utilised civil and canon law

---

[1] The text of a lecture delivered on 20 September 2012 at the 66th Session of the *Société Internationale pour l'Histoire des Droits de l'Antiquité* (Oxford, 18–22 September 2012).

[2] J. Beatson and R. Zimmermann (eds.), *Jurists Uprooted: German-speaking Émigré Lawyers in Twentieth-century Britain* (Oxford, 2004).

to deal with ecclesiastical matters and litigation involving international trade – almost a third of these lawyers came from Wales. Many of these were also frequently employed by the Tudor monarchs on diplomatic missions abroad, including some of those who had held the Regius chair at Oxford, which until the time of Gentili, who had also been employed as a diplomat, has the appearance of being a stepping-stone to later judicial eminence and political preferment.

The predominance of Welshmen in the learning of civil and canon law in Tudor England invites a number of questions, one of which I wish to examine this morning, namely how deep were the roots of this civilian and canonical learning in Wales before the union with England, how far back in the legal history of Wales can the influence of civil law be detected. Prior to the union with England, Welshmen as foreigners could not ordinarily have been admitted as lawyers before the royal courts at Westminster,[3] but there was nothing to prevent them from being admitted as advocates and proctors to practise before the courts of the Western church. Thus, for instance, we know that among the ecclesiastical supporters of the revolt of Owain Glyn Dŵr against the English king, Henry IV, in the first decade of the fifteenth century were numbered Lewis Byford, the bishop of Bangor, John Trefor, the bishop of St Asaph, and Gruffydd Young, the archdeacon of Meirionydd, all three of whom were trained canonists, with Trefor having served at the Papal Curia before his appointment to the diocese of St Asaph in north-east Wales.[4] There appears therefore to have been a tradition of canonical and indeed civilian learning in Wales prior to the accession of the Tudor kings, before the union with England and therefore

---

[3] There were exceptions; most notably perhaps David Hanmer who became a Serjeant at law (1371), a King's Serjeant (1377–83) and a Justice of the Court of King's Bench (1383–87). His effigy in his judicial robes can be seen in Gresford parish church. His daughter married Owain Glyn Dŵr, who is believed to have attended the Inns of Court but more as a sort of finishing school than with a view to legal practice. Interestingly, two other serjeants with seemingly Welsh names were also created towards the end of Edward III's reign – Thomas Moris and Wiliam Rys, both in 1362. The Glyn Dŵr revolt may have closed this career path to aspiring Welshmen, although by the end of the fifteenth century grants of denizen status to individuals in return for loyal service, or even to whole communities, were becoming more frequent: see T.G. Watkin, *The Legal History of Wales* (2nd ed., Cardiff, 2012), pp. 118–119, 121–122, 125–126.

[4] See Watkin, *Legal History*, p. 116–117.

before the foundation of Jesus College here in Oxford, where later generations of Welsh civilians were to receive their education, among them the notable seventeenth-century Welsh civilian Leoline Jenkins, who lies buried before the altar in the college chapel.

The civilian learning among the Welsh of the Tudor period extended even beyond the ranks of the scholars, professors and advocates whose learning primarily involved a knowledge of civil law. Shortly after Gentili's appointment to the Regius chair here in Oxford, a very significant event occurred in the history of Wales, for in 1588, the work of producing a Welsh translation of the Bible from the original languages was completed, the Bible usually known as that of Bishop William Morgan, the principal translator and also a bishop of St Asaph, the Bible which ensured the transmission to future generations not only the Christian faith of their forebears but also a standard, literary form of their native language. It was the Bible which preserved Welsh as a living language, and whereas the standard English of later centuries was that of the royal court – the King's or the Queen's English, standard Welsh was that of the Bible – *Cymraeg y Beibl*.

In his translation of the eleventh chapter of St Luke's gospel, Bishop Morgan provides a version in Welsh of Our Lord's teaching on prayer, including what is sometimes referred to as the parable of the importunate friend. In modern English, the passage reads:

> "Suppose one of you has a friend who comes to you in the middle of the night and says, 'My friend, lend me three loaves, for a friend of mine on a journey has turned up at my house, and I have nothing to offer him'".[5]

Now, a law teacher – perhaps in particular a teacher of the civil law – reading that passage is likely to ask himself – or even his students – 'What kind of loan was this? Was it a loan for safe-keeping, a loan for use or a

[5] Luke, 11. vv. 5–6. The Welsh translation by Bishop William Morgan (1588) reads:

> Ac efe a ddywedodd wrthynt, Pwy o honoch fydd iddo gyfaill, ac a â atto hanner nos, ac a ddywed wrtho, O gyfaill, moes i mi dair torth yn echwyn;
>
> Canys gyfaill i mi addaeth attaf wrth ymdaith, ac nid oes gennyf ddim i'w ddodi ger ei fron ef;

loan for consumption? *Depositum*, *commodatum* or *mutuum*? Today, one could not perhaps expect a Biblical translator to ask that question, but things were clearly different in sixteenth-century Wales for Bishop William Morgan clearly did ask it, and moreover answered it correctly, for in his Welsh translation, he identifies the loan as one for consumption, *mutuum*, and uses the equivalent term in Welsh, *echwyn* – 'O gyfaill, moes i mi dair torth yn echwyn'. Just in case you think I am being unfair on modern translators, I feel obliged to point out that the modern Welsh translation of the passage, published in 1988, misses the point and uses the Welsh word *benthyg*, 'to borrow', but which in the native laws of Wales meant 'borrowing for use' not 'borrowing for consumption'. For good measure, it is worth perhaps noting that the Latin of the Vulgate renders the request, 'commoda mihi tres panes', also seemingly confusing *mutuum* and *commodatum*, albeit perhaps following the Greek original where the general word for lending, *χρήσον* from *κιχρημι*, is used rather than any more technical legal term. In this, the Greek of the New Testament is very like English – there is no dedicated term which makes the legal distinction as is the case in Latin, where the language captures the sophistication of the legal analysis.

Therein, of course, lies the significance of Bishop William Morgan's translation, for Morgan carefully chose the Welsh word *echwyn* which corresponded exactly to the Latin word *mutuum*, and he was able to do that because there was present in Welsh a legal vocabulary which corresponded to the Latin, in other words an equivalent register of legal terminology.

This gives rise to the question of the extent to which the legal register in Welsh corresponded to that in Latin. In the time available this morning, one example – albeit a very good one – will have to suffice, but it should be sufficient to illustrate the correspondence in terminology, a correspondence which reflects a legal analysis of borrowing transactions which is not merely similar to, but virtually identical with, that of Roman law, which will give rise to the question of how this came to be. The correspondence relates to the area which has already been the focus of the discussion, namely the obligations which arise from real contracts.

The civilian analysis of such obligations is as perhaps as well-known as it is simple in its sophistication and for that reason aesthetically pleasing. Distinctions are drawn between loans for use (*commodatum*), consumption (*mutuum*), safe-keeping (*depositum*) and security (*pignus*).[6] Aside from the attempt of Bracton in the thirteenth century to impose this civilian sophistication upon the nascent common law,[7] English law remained largely immune from a logical analysis of this sort until Holt CJ felt obliged to return to Bracton's example and borrow the civilian analysis in order to achieve an ordered exposition of the common law relating to these obligations in the case of *Coggs* v *Bernard* at the start of the eighteenth century.[8]

That however was not true of the native laws of Wales, where the full rigour of the Roman analysis can be seen in the law texts dating from half a millennium earlier.[9] The native laws knew, recognized and used the self-same distinctions as the Roman jurists. As Bishop William Morgan recognized in his translation of the passage from St Luke's gospel discussed earlier, a loan for consumption was different from a loan for use. Borrowing three loaves of bread was the former not the latter, and the vocabulary of Welsh in the sixteenth century reflected the legal terminology of, at least, the preceding four centuries in describing the loan for consumption as *echwyn*, while the loan for use was *benthyg*. Interestingly, modern Welsh uses the latter term indiscriminately, like *borrow* in English, perhaps as a result of the gradual demise of the native jurisprudence and its terminology following the extension of the English common law to the whole of Wales as a consequence of the legal and political union accomplished by the Tudors.

The Welsh laws also recognized a distinct loan for safe keeping, *adneu*, and the giving of an item of personal property as security for a loan or debt, *gwystl*. Very interestingly, with regard to the latter, the rules relating to the return of such items reflect some of the Biblical injunctions against taking advantage of or oppressing a debtor.[10]

---

[6] The Roman category of real contracts is described for instance in Justinian's *Institutes*, III.14. The classification continues in many modern codes of civil law.

[7] Bracton, *De Legibus et Consuetudinibus Angliae*, f. 99.

[8] *Coggs* v *Bernard* (1703) 2 Ld. Raymond 909.

[9] See for example A. R. Wiliam, *Llyfr Iorwerth*, (Cardiff, 1960), ¶¶ 113, 124; H.D. Emanuel, *The Latin Texts of the Welsh Laws* (Cardiff, 1967), 124–125 (*Latin A*), 258 (*Latin B*), 376–377 (*Latin D*).

[10] See T.G. Watkin, 'Cyfraith Cymru', in Tegid Roberts (ed.), *Yr Angen am Furiau: Pum Darlith Fforwm Hanes Cymru* (Llanrwst, 2009), pp. 64–80; English

The similarity in the analysis does not end with the civilian classification of real contracts; it extends also to the manner in which these are distinguished from other agreements. Thus, the gratuitous loan for use (*benthyg*) was distinguished from the hire of a thing in return for payment, the Roman *locatio/conductio*. In the laws of mediaeval Wales, such an arrangement was described as *llog*, a term which is believed to have been itself borrowed from the Latin *locatio*. The essence of that distinction lies in the gratuitous nature of the former as contrasted with the mercenary element in the latter, the former being viewed as a transaction motivated by friendship, *amicitia*, rather than gain or advantage. Interestingly, lending for use is sometimes described as *cymwyn*, a term close to *cymwynas*, meaning 'a favour' or 'a good turn'. In this sense, *cymwyn* describes what the lender does as opposed to what the borrower does, *benthyg*, introducing that duality of description which marks some of the Roman consensual contracts, *emptio/venditio* (sale) as well as *locatio/conductio* (hire). It is also the case that this usage of *cymwyn* mirrors the use of *commoda* in the Latin Vulgate version of the parable of the importunate friend, although there is no accepted etymological connection between the two words as there is with *llog* and *locatio*.[11]

The mediaeval laws of Wales, in which these conceptual and terminological resemblances occur, are traditionally ascribed to the legal activity of the tenth-century prince, Hywel Dda, under whose rule much of what is now Wales was united. Although his legal activity is ascribed to the first half of the tenth century, the earliest extant manuscript evidence for the laws promulgated by him comes from the twelfth century. Hywel is said to have gathered clerical and lay representatives of the lands over which he ruled to an assembly at Whitland in south-west Wales where his laws were promulgated. Many believe that this assembly served as a meeting at which the pre-existing customs of the various parts of Wales were recorded and set down in writing, so that Hywel was less of a law maker than a codifier of customs. What is definitely known is that the laws ascribed to him were regarded as the source of the laws which continued to govern the native inhabitants of Wales for several centuries thereafter, in

---

version – 'The Laws of Wales' in T.G. Watkin (ed.), *The Carno Poisonings and Other Essays* (Bangor, 2013), pp. 33–48.

[11] See the entries for *llog* and *cymwyn* in *Geiriadur Prifysgol Cymru: A Dictionary of the Welsh Language* (Cardiff, 1950–2002).

some cases right down to the union with England in the sixteenth century. Although regional divergences occurred, and the laws were revised from time to time, the mediaeval laws of Wales were always regarded as the laws of Hywel, providing in their written, legal tradition a focus of unity for the people of Wales.

This background poses some questions for the facts considered earlier. Were the conceptual and terminological similarities identified earlier between the mediaeval laws of Wales and Roman civil law, were those similarities present in Hywel's own compilations or were they introduced in later revisions, and if they were present in Hywel's original compilations, for how long had they existed in the customs of Wales? Basically, this question is whether the laws of mediaeval Wales contained survivals of a Romanism from an earlier age or whether they reflect the results of a later civilian influence which, Bracton apart, would appear to have been more strongly felt in Wales than in its eastern neighbour.

At first blush, the idea of the similarities being a survival of the Roman period in British history appears far-fetched, and there is of course virtually no written evidence – certainly insufficient written evidence – to support such a theory. However, that is not to say that there is no evidence at all. Evidence of continuity in the lives of the native inhabitants between the Roman and sub-Roman periods abounds. It is known, for instance, that the native inhabitants continued to use the roads built by the Romans, and that they continued to occupy settlements and build afresh upon sites which had been developed by the Romans. In particular, churches were built close to Roman settlements and near Roman roads. Mining and trading activities begun by the Romans were also continued, trade being particularly common with those parts of mainland Europe which endeavoured to maintain their Roman cultural heritage despite the fall of the western empire. Fierce retention of such cultural Romanism was also a feature of the native British; the sixth-century writer, Gildas, bemoaned the effects of Saxon influence upon what he described as *nostra lingua*, by which he meant Latin, and that was still the chosen language for many epitaphs on the graves of leaders, whose credentials to govern were routinely presented in terms of a distinguished line of descent which connected them with their Roman predecessors. Rome was still regarded by the British as the true fount of legitimate authority, and, in the face of the Anglo-Saxon incursions which created the English kingdoms, they continued until the twelfth century to refer to themselves as *Brythaniaid* and to refer to their land as *Britannia*. Many Latin words formed linguistic roots in the emerging Welsh language. Above all, the native British jealously guarded the greatest legacy of the period of Roman rule, their Christian faith. Above all else, this marked them apart from the pagan English settlers, and they fiercely defended their cultural Romanism of which the faith was the central part. A combination of Christian and classical learning was provided to the young at monastic schools, such as that at Llanilltud Fawr in the Vale of Glamorgan (the English Llantwit Major), where the classical element in the curriculum included poetry, grammar, rhetoric and arithmetic, a form of education which was still on offer when the Normans arrived in south Wales. Against such a background, the possibility of legal survivals ceases to be so far-fetched, and from the first evidence extant of the legal culture of the Welsh, it is markedly different from that of its eastern neighbour in its emphasis upon written law rather than custom, and the use of law books by trained jurists in the resolution of disputes, again markedly civilian perspectives.

The other possibility with regard to the civilian elements in the Welsh laws is that they were introduced later, as elements of the revived Roman legal learning found its way to Wales. This would tie the development very closely with the period from which written evidence has survived, for the first manuscripts containing texts of the native laws come from the twelfth and thirteenth centuries, the period immediately following the absorption of the Christian Church in Wales into the diocesan structure of the Province of Canterbury of which the Welsh Church now became a part. This was, of course, also the period which saw the emergence of canon law as a subject of study in the law schools of mainland Europe and ultimately in the law faculties at Oxford and Cambridge as well. Clerics who served in Wales are known to have availed themselves of this new learning, as witness the legal campaigns of Giraldus Cambrensis and others during the twelfth century to establish the four dioceses of the Welsh Church as a province separate from that of Canterbury, with St David's in west Wales as the metropolitical see. The campaigns were unsuccessful, but the presence of sound canonical learning fuelling them is fully evidenced. The involvement of ecclesiastics trained in the learned laws in the production of the surviving manuscripts of the mediaeval Welsh laws is not open to serious doubt, and it is tempting to see here another avenue by which civilian learning and terminology might have crept into the native jurisprudence. Were that the only route, however, it is strange many of the terms for the civilian concepts are not more closely related to the Latin, as with *locatio* and *llog*. The presence of an alternative terminology would suggest that the concepts if not the analysis itself may have come from an earlier period, although it is also plausible that encountering native terms similar in meaning to the civilian terminology, it was decided by the compilers to retain them in deference to their familiarity.

At the end of the day, it is probably false to suggest that one needs to make a choice between the two scenarios, between, that is, survivals from the Roman period and the incorporation of civilian elements by trained canonists following the rebirth of Roman legal studies. Just as there is insufficient evidence to advocate one of these views at the expense of the other, so too there is insufficient evidence to reject either in its entirety.

There is, of course, a third possibility, one that would reject any degree of civilian influence at all and assert that the similarities are a complete coincidence, that the native Welsh concepts were achieved entirely independently of any contact with Roman jurisprudence. On the basis of the conceptual and terminological evidence presented this morning, which is only a part of the picture with regard to such similarities, that is the possibility which I would invite you to reject, and thereby recognize that there is indeed a legitimate field of inquiry regarding the extent of civilian influence on the native laws of Wales and the route by which that influence came to be felt.

Diolch yn fawr. Thank you very much.

WELSH WAR HORSES IN NEWTOWN

A Case from World War One

Dr. Rachael Jones

MICHAEL Morpurgo's book *War Horse* has been phenomenal in informing the public about the role of horses in the First World War.[1] In the story, the animal originated in Devon and saw service on the western front. In reality, horses such as this numbered hundreds of thousands, having been drawn into the conflict for draft work or as so-called 'remounts', trained and shipped across to the continent.[2] The Montgomeryshire and Welsh Horse Yeomanry regiments played a part in this, and their mobilisation and progress through Wales, with associated billeting needs, led to the prosecution of a disgruntled innkeeper at Newtown Police Court. The case forms the subject of this essay, and gives an insight into the effect of visiting soldiers on local economics.[3]

Background to the case

While for many years war horses had been brought over to mainland Britain from Ireland, the government made efforts to encourage the improvement of home-reared stock.[4] An 1888 Royal Commission gave

---

[1] M. Morpurgo, *War Horse* (London, 1982).

[2] For background information see J. Singleton, 'Britain's military use of horses, 1914–18', (1993) 139 *Past & Present,* 178–203. See also B. Scott, *Galloper Jack* (London, 2003) for the true story of Jack Seely who served in the Hampshire Yeomanry during the Boer War and then in World War 1. See also S. Butler, *The War Horses* (Wellington, 2001); J. Seely, *Warrior: The Amazing Story of a Real War Horse* (Newbury, 2011).

[3] The history of the Montgomeryshire Yeomanry is detailed in R.W. Williams Wynn & W.N. Stable, *The Historical Records of the Montgomeryshire Yeomanry, 1909–1919* (Wrexham, 1926).

[4] In the 1890s, the sale of horses to the British added over £1 million to the Irish economy: see F.M.L. Thompson, 'Nineteenth-century horse sense', (1976) 29 *The Economic History Review*, 78.

grants to owners of good thoroughbred stallions which resulted in the government subsidizing horse breeding by £5,000 during the first years of the twentieth century.[5] These efforts could be observed in Montgomeryshire in, for example, the Montgomeryshire Entire Horse Association, which loaned out stallions to farmers for a small fee, or the Gregynog Estate Improvement Society which hired a stallion from late Prime Minister William Gladstone's Flintshire estate.[6] At the same time, the British army established a remount department and created a horsc reserve. Here owners registered their animals, promising to sell them to the army in the event of war. Despite these efforts, during the Boer war of 1899-1902,[7] about three quarters of all remounts were bought overseas from countries including Australia, USA, Argentina and Canada. The experiences of the mounted divisions during the war in South Africa was poor, with horses being sent to field units without adequate time being allowed for adjustment to foreign conditions. Furthermore, British troops had not properly appreciated the different temperaments and dietary needs of animals from overseas.[8] Now, in 1914, with Britain newly at war with Germany, efforts were made to avoid the same mistakes.[9] For example, training of local cavalry was carried out in Welshpool at the *Coed y Dinas* field, lent by the Earl of Powis, with regular inspections by visiting high-

---

[5] Singleton, 'Britain's military use', pp.178–183. See also Collins, E.J.T., 'The farm horse economy of England and Wales in the Early Tractor Age', in Thompson, F.M.L., *Horses in European economic history: A Preliminary Canter* (Reading, 1983), pp.73–100.

[6] See R. Jones, 'The Leighton and Brynllywarch Estates: William Scott Owen's records', in P. Barton (ed.), (2010) 98 *The Montgomeryshire Collections*, 103–4; R. Jones 'The Gregynog Estate, 1880–1920 (unpublished M.A. dissertation, copy at Newtown (Powys) Library), Chapters 3 and 4.

[7] See 'Boer Wars' in J. Cannon (ed.), *The Oxford Companion to British History* (Oxford, 1997, 2002), p. 110.

[8] S. Jones, 'Horses in the Anglo-Boer War', *BBC History* (Feb. 2014), p. 32.

[9] For a review of the availability of horses in Germany, showing how the number had increased dramatically by 1913, see A. Kander and P. Warde, 'Number, size and energy consumption of draught animals in European agriculture', available at http://www.histecon.magd.cam.ac.uk/history-sust/files/warde_kander_working_paper_animals-mar09.pdf (viewed 4/11/2013).

ranking officers. Figure 1 shows the Yeomanry watering their horses near Welshpool.

Figure 1: The Montgomeryshire Yeomanry, near Welshpool.[10]

The Montgomeryshire Yeomanry and a large contingency of Canadian horses were involved in this training, with the officers being billeted at the Royal Oak Hotel in the town, and the men at houses. Their presence undoubtedly brought money into the area, for as well as the compensation paid by the government to householders and hoteliers for billeting, the men spent their pay around town. The presence of the horses also meant work for farriers, saddlers, harness makers and a range of other craftsmen.[11] When mayor Thomas Evans was encouraging the rest of the town council

---

[10] Reproduced courtesy of the Powysland Museum, Welshpool. The picture appears in E. B. Bredesdorff, *Welshpool in Old Photographs*, (Stroud, 1993), p. 145. Detailed examination of the cap badge, showing a dragon, confirms that this is the Montgomery Yeomanry. The photograph is undated but the uniform puts it at the time of the First World War.

[11] Thompson, 'Horse sense', p. 78.

to consider providing more stabling, he said: 'I am sure you are all desirous of doing so, as the men spent a good deal of money there'. Horses were stabled at the Smithfield although they had to vacate this location on market days during which time they were accommodated in the stables of local hotels.[12] A disused flannel factory on Salop Road was used, for which, no doubt, the owner was compensated. Differentials could result in envy shown, for example when some Welshpool householders claimed that the allowance of 14 shillings per man per week was not enough when the rate in Newtown was a shilling per week more.[13]

In Newtown there were nearly 400 members of the Welsh Horse Yeomanry staying all around the town by the middle of February 1915,[14] bringing in about £300 every week just from the billeting of the men at the rate quoted previously.[15] More would have come from the stabling of their horses at the government rate of 12s. 3d per week.[16] This regiment was a force that had been raised initially in Cardiff but was transferred to Montgomeryshire. *The South Wales Echo* enquired:

> The Welsh Horse, which originated in Cardiff, which was raised in Cardiff, which was provided with nearly all its equipment by Cardiff people, is not now to have its depot in Cardiff. The depot has been collared from Cardiff by Newtown. Not 10 percent of the troopers come from North Wales, and I believe I am right in saying that not a ten pound note was subscribed in North Wales towards the funds. When the army comes marching home again, which I hope to goodness will not be many months hence, the Welsh Horse will return, not to the city which gave it birth, but

---

[12] *The County Times*, 31/10/1914.
[13] *The County Times*, 16/1/1915.
[14] *The County Times*, 13/2/1915
[15] As a comparison, an advertisement in *The County Times* dated 13 March 1915 shows that a Ford motor car cost £125, and Newtown Urban District Council spent the same amount on street cleaning across a whole year. Powys County Archives, *Newtown Urban District Council minute book*, item no. M/UD/NL/15.
[16] The rate was quoted during the forthcoming court case and reported in *The County Times*, 16/1/1916. F.M.L. Thompson states that at the very beginning of the twentieth century, the weekly cost of feeding a town horse was about 10 shillings. ('Nineteenth-century horse sense', p. 78).

> to a part of the Principality with which nine tenths of them have no association and nothing to remind them of the days when they were, so to speak, nursed for the time when they should serve their king and country.[17]

Although the reasons for their removal to Newtown are said to be unknown,[18] when the first batch of men and horses arrived at the end of December 1914, *The County Times* reported that: 'the council decided to thank the general manager of the Cambrian Railways for his good offices in regard to the headquarters of the Welsh Horse Yeomanry, which had no doubt resulted in the selection of Newtown by the authorities'.[19] This could be a reference to the land lying between the railway line and the Welshpool road which later became the site of the town's horse repository and cattle market.[20] However, there may have been a political factor to their reassignment to Montgomeryshire, for mentioned in passing in Bryn Owen's *Owen Roscomyl and the Welsh Horse* and in *The County Times* is the fact that officers were billeted with David Davies, Liberal Member of Parliament for Montgomeryshire,[21] at *Broneirion*, a few miles from the town.[22] Davies may well have identified an opportunity to aid the fortunes of the town which had been struggling for years.[23] Indeed, in early December 1914, *The County Times* reported:

---

[17] B. Owen, *Owen Roscomyl and the Welsh Horse* (Caernarfon, 1990), p. 29. See also B. Owen, *History of the Welsh Militia and Volunteer Force* (Wrexham, 2000).
[18] Owen, *Roscomyl*, p. 29.
[19] *The County Times*, 9/1/1915.
[20] See reports of the urban district council's discussions on plans for a horse repository in *The County Times* January to March 1915.
[21] 'David Davies' in *D.N.B.*
[22] Owen, *Roscomyl,* p. 39 and, for example, *The County Times*, 6/1/1915 which details a road accident suffered by commanding officer Lord Kenyon on his way to Newtown from *Broneirion*.
[23] The rise and fall of the flannel industry in Mid Wales is well documented, see for example J. Moreton Pearson, 'The decayed and decaying industries of Montgomeryshire', (1915), 37 *The Montgomeryshire Collections*, 15–30 (written at the time of the event under discussion here, concluding with the comment that the county was largely agricultural as most of the industry had gone). See also J. Geraint Jenkins, 'The woollen industry in Montgomeryshire', (1963–64) 58 *The*

> Just as Newtown people were mourning the loss of the Royal Welch Fusiliers[24] for Aberystwyth, rumours were afloat that in the town that there might be some substantial compensation for this loss. The rumour was that the reserve regiment of the Welsh Horse which is now being raised by Lord Kenyon from the six North Wales counties would be trained in Newtown.[25]

The tip off may have originated from David Davies himself as the article ended:

> We hear on good authority that in the event of Newtown being selected, a gentleman living outside Newtown has offered him [Lord Kenyon] the use of his property.

The non-commissioned officers and other men were billeted around town, where the decayed and disadvantaged nature of the area was reflected in the lack of basic amenities in many of the houses. Local doctor Frederick Wilson reported to the town council: 'There have been complaints from the Welsh Horse of the small number of baths in the billets. Could we ask that the residents of the town who have baths to make a loan of them for the use of the horsemen?' A discussion then ensued including a suggestion that a temporary bathhouse might be made out of an empty building which was discounted because providing hot water to this would be problematic. Eventually it was decided that householders would be approached for the loan of baths.[26]

Despite the lack of facilities, a tone of revelry seemed apparent amongst the horsemen and residents of the town. For example, a committee was formed to arrange concerts, dances and football matches. Boxing exhibitions took place, given by the several professional boxers who had

---

Montgomeryshire Collections, 50–69. There is an excellent discussion in an editorial 'The population in Newtown in 1871', *Newtown and Welshpool Express*, 23/4/1871. The disused flannel factory used for army horses in Welshpool mentioned earlier is an example of the fortuitous recycling that was possible during the stationing of the Yeomanry in the area.

[24] 'Welch' was the accepted spelling in the title of this branch of the armed forces.

[25] *The County Times*, 12/12/1914.

[26] *The County Times*, 15/1/1915.

been recruited. The proceeds from these functions were said to be 'devoted to the regiment and the benefit of the town'.[27] It is notable that the regiment's arrival was during the midwinter months when activities to fill the long evening hours would have been at a premium.

Events leading to the prosecution

Newtown was swamped with horses. Surplus Canadian animals may have passed through the town after they were removed from Welshpool, and 100 equines arrived from Ormskirk in January 1915. At a rate of a little over 12 shillings per week per horse, the Lancashire animals alone would have brought in about £60 per week. It was the accommodation of nearly half of them that was problematic for one innkeeper who claimed that the level of remuneration was not enough. The first sign of trouble was when the inn, the Black Boy, situated on the main shopping street, was made out of bounds to reservists. The inn is shown in Figure 2. The order was given without warning, and men whose horses were stabled there were commanded to remove them. One trooper said, "I was coming over the bridge with my girl when somebody came up to me and said, 'Hurry up, get your horse out.' I thought the Germans had come here at last."[28]

The reason for the evacuation from the inn became apparent on 14 January 1915 when John Williams appeared at a special sessions, before magistrates Richard Lloyd and Edward Morgan. He was charged with a breach of the 1881 Army Act, by refusing to accommodate 42 animals.[29]

---

[27] *The County Times,* 30/1/1915.
[28] *The County Times*, 23/1/1915.
[29] *The County Times*, 16/1/1915 and *The Montgomeryshire Express*, 19/1/1915. The relevant section of the Act reads: Whereas by Section 108A of the Army Act it is amongst other things enacted that where directions have been given for embodying all or any part of the Territorial Force it shall be lawful for His Majesty, by Order distinctly stating that a case of emergency exists, and signified by a Secretary of State, to authorise any General or Field Officer Commanding any part of His Majesty's Forces in any military district or place in the United Kingdom to issue a Billeting Requisition under his hand, requiring Chief Officers of Police to provide billets in such places and for such number of officers and soldiers and their horses and for such period as may be specified in the Requisition in accordance with the provisions of the said Section. See 'Proclamations that

He pleaded not guilty, and the prosecution case was brought by the police, represented by Sergeant David Davies. Also present was a representative of the owners of the inn, Ind Coope and Company. The proceedings began with Sgt Davies describing how the trouble began.

Figure 2: The Black Boy Inn, Broad Street, Newtown
(courtesy of Newtown Local History Group)

Sgt Davies: At about 11 o'clock on Monday morning [11 January] I was requisitioned by Lieutenant Williams, adjutant of the Welsh Horse, to billet 100 horses. 42 were to go to the Black Boy, 12 to the Blue Bell, 16 to the Unicorn, 12 to the Sun Inn and 17 to the Buck Hotel. Lieut. Williams asked me to go round to the innkeepers to warn them to be in readiness and to have forage ready. I went to the Black

---

mobilised the army' viewed at www.1914-1918.net (6/11/2013).

> Boy Inn, kept by the defendant, and told him that there were 42 horses coming there that evening, and he was to stable them and find forage. Williams said, 'No, I am not going to find forage for them.' I told him he was bound to do so and he said, 'No, I am not bound to do so as long as I haven't got any. If I haven't got the money you don't want me to go and pinch it to get forage.' I told him I was not there to argue, but to tell him that he must find forage. I then left the premises.

The sergeant explained that he returned to the inn at about 7.30 that evening and received a complaint from one of the men in charge of the horses that the animals were overcrowded.[30] There was a stable lying empty but Williams would not allow any horses to be moved into it. Sgt Davies ordered the removal of two horses from the overcrowded stable to the empty one, and again left the premises. Figure 3 shows a plan of the Black Boy and its outbuildings and stables.

The matter did not rest there, however, and the following day new complaints were received indicating that Williams was not providing adequate feed. When the sergeant returned with an army officer, he claimed that Williams again spoke of money:

> Sgt Davies: Williams said, 'can't do it, I can't afford to do it.' I told him that he was bound to do so and that he must find forage. He again said, 'You don't want me to pinch money to get fodder for them, do you?' and I also told him that I knew he had been using bad language towards the sergeant major.'

---

[30] In 1915 the Our Dumb Friends League (now the Blue Cross) issued *The Drivers, Gunners' and mounted soldiers' Handbook to Management and Care of Horses and Harness*. One section reads: 'A driver should make it his business to see that his horses get the usual amounts and not a bit less. A driver will incur no reprimand if he reports to his sergeant any suspected deficiency.' 'Blue Cross War Horse Collection' viewed at www.bluecross.org.uk (viewed 13/11/2013).

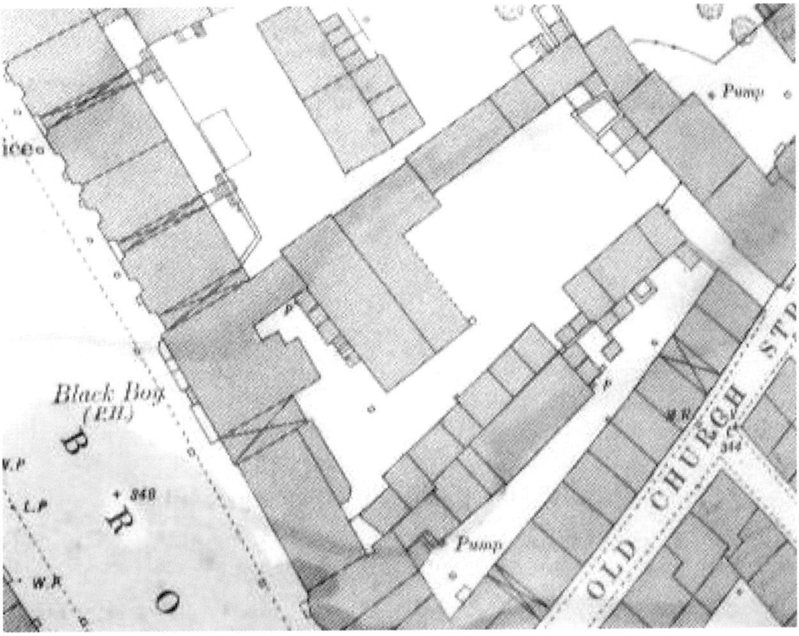

Figure 3: Plan of the Black Boy Inn,
from 6 inch Ordnance Survey map of Newtown (1884)[31]

This claim of bad language was to be returned to later, but for the present, it was the turn of the defence as lawyer William George asked questions of the police officer.[32]

George:	What is the exact offence with which you charge him?
Sgt Davies:	Neglecting to provide sufficient food for the horses.
George:	You know that all along he has said that he could not find the money to get provender for the horses?
Sgt Davies:	Yes
George:	It takes a good deal of money to provide 42 horses with fodder and litter

---

31 Held at Newtown (Powys) Public Library.

32 The solicitor may have been Richard Edward George, younger brother of William, as the precise identity is unclear.

Sgt Davies:	It does
George:	How much do you think it costs?
Sgt Davies:	The Government allows 12s. 3d. per week per horse. For the defendant that would come to roughly £25 a week

The questioning went on to elicit that the sergeant had not served written notice on Mr Williams, but had only given verbal instructions. The army man claimed that written notice was given only in emergencies. Mr George's questioning now turned to threats that had been made:

George:	He was threatened with being locked up and turned out of the house, wasn't he?
Davies:	Certainly. He was very insolent. He was under the influence of drink
George:	You took for billeting every available stall that this man had?
Davies:	I think there were one or two left

Here the clerk interjected: 'Did you threaten to lock him up?' Davies replied, 'I told him he was liable to be locked up.' The police sergeant also said, in reply to other questions, that he had visited the Black Boy Inn about a month previously to enquire into the number of animals he could accommodate. On being told that the number was 42, he put the defendant down for that number.

At this point in the trial, former professional boxer James Driscoll entered in the witness box.[33] He explained that it was his duty to visit the horses and check on the care of the animals. He had already inspected the Black Boy stables several times on Tuesday 12 January and when he returned at about 5pm, he observed the defendant measuring out feeds. In his opinion, they were not sufficient.

Driscoll:	There was enough chaff and bran but not sufficient oats. I did not weigh the oats but I could see that the defendant added a little from a can. I told him I did

[33] For a biography of James Driscoll see 'Peerless James Driscoll' viewed at http://www.bbc.co.uk/blogs/blogwales/posts/peerless_jim_driscoll_welsh_boxer (viewed 5/11/2013).

	not believe there was sufficient oats but he told me he knew his business. I reported the matter to the sergeant major.
George:	May I ask you what you were engaged in before you joined the army? Had you anything to do with horses?
Driscoll:	Yes, a little.
George:	Then you found something a little more profitable?
Driscoll:	Yes

Driscoll's last response was greeted by laughter in the court. Mr George's questioning went on:

George:	Did the defendant complain to you that it was very difficult to find the money?
Driscoll:	He did.
George:	Did he tell you that he had been up in the middle of the night attending to two horses which had got loose?
Driscoll:	I don't think so.

The next witness to take the stand was Sergeant-Major Daniel Morgan who described how he went to the Black Boy on the Tuesday evening, in consequence of Driscoll's report. He watched feed being put into buckets and given to the men for their horses. He told the magistrates:

Morgan:	I examined them and saw that they were very inadequate. I asked the defendant whether he thought that what he was serving was sufficient food for horses. He turned round and used the most filthy and offensive language.
Sgt Davies:	What did you say then?
Morgan:	I told him I was there to see that the proper feeds were given to the horses, as there had been complaints. I told him the feed he was giving was just not sufficient.
Sgt Davies:	What did the defendant say to that?
Morgan;	He said that he knew his business and told me to clear out and to do what the ---- I liked. He got into such a raving passion that it was useless to argue with him at the time.
Sgt Davies:	Did you say anything else?

Morgan:	I asked him if he was going to put any more oats in and he replied 'No, not a ----- bit more. I'll see you in ----- first. I have done my time in the service and have met such as you before.'
Sgt Davies:	What did you do then?
Morgan:	I took a bucket from one of the men and took it to show the officers. Afterwards I took it to the police with instructions to proceed.
Clerk:	What did you complain about?
Morgan:	Insufficient food. There is a lot of chaff in the bottom of the bucket. I take it there's not a pound of oats there. There's a little bran, the buckets about three parts full of chaff.[34]

Morgan then went on to explain how the proportions of different types of feed were usually calculated. He then took questions from defence lawyer Mr George.

George:	You say no hay was dealt out that night?
Morgan:	No
George:	As a matter of fact Mr Williams bought hay that day, and here's the receipt. I don't suppose he ate it himself.
Morgan:	It was reported to me that no hay was issued that night.
George:	Did the defendant say it was hard for him to find the money to purchase the forage?
Morgan:	No. If he had done so perhaps I should have taken a different view of the case. If he hadn't

[34] Chaff in equine feed terminology is chopped hay. Mixing chaff with other grains has one main purpose: it forces the horse to chew more thoroughly. Oats was the staple feed for equines because it was readily available, cheap and, most importantly, best suited to their digestive systems. Oats has the highest fibre content and lowest energy of all the grains, making it the safest to feed. The grain size also meant that horses can chew them effectively, maximising their goodness. Bran is light in weight – a full scoop only weighs about half a pound – so it can be added at low levels to bulk out a diet without compromising the nutrient supply, and it has about the same energy content as modern competition feeds. www.horseandhound.co.uk (viewed 1/2/2014).

> used such abusive language to me it would have been different for him. He could find the money to buy drink; I'm a staunch teetotaller myself.

Sergeant William Henry Ellson appeared before the magistrates next and told them that he thought Williams seemed to be confused, hurrying over giving out feeds on the Tuesday evening, apparently trying to prevent him from inspecting the buckets full of fodder. However, he did concede that the morning feeds had been very good. Police Sergeant Davies continued to question him.

Sgt Davies:	On Monday night you had some trouble with Mr Williams?
Ellson:	Yes. He kept me there until 9.30 fiddling about with the horses when I might have gone at 8.30.
Sgt Davies:	Did he know what was required of him?
Ellson:	He told me he knew the routine. He had been an old soldier and knew all the tricks of the trade. He seemed to know the Billeting Act better that I did, and I have been billeting now for 22 years.[35]

Now Mr George took over the questioning:

George:	You say he was confused on Tuesday?
Ellson:	I think he had a drop of drink. It was market day and I think he had a drop too much. That's my opinion of it.
George:	You congratulated him on the morning and afternoon feeds?
Ellson:	Yes. He supplied as good a class of oats as any in the town.
George:	What you think is that he was probably a bit mixed up at the time?
Ellson:	My opinion is that the bag was running short, that the defendant had not calculated properly what he would require and was trying to make that bag last till morning.
George:	You didn't see him weigh out the feeds?

[35] See 'billeting' in Cannon, *The Oxford Companion*, pp. 102–3.

Ellson:	No, he told me that a box he had held three pounds and a little more.
George:	Did he tell you that he couldn't find the money?
Ellson:	Yes. The horses had been pushed on him.

Sergeant Ellson's testimony concluded the case for the Prosecution, and now Mr George began to plead on his client's behalf. He explained that Williams had been accommodating soldiers since the outbreak of the war. He knew he was supposed to find provender for the animals but it was very difficult as remuneration took a long time to arrive, and it was a very large outlay for him. Mr George went on:

George: How many of the innkeepers of this town, and he was sorry to say it, could find such a great lump of money to provide for forage? They could not get the goods at any shop without cash. The defendant on Tuesday was undoubtedly a little upset. The fact that Sgt Ellson congratulated him on some of the feeds was something in his favour to show that he was not trying tricks on the government. Their worships would know how much forage etc. could be got for 12s 3d a week per horse. My client did not refuse to provide the forage but said that the amount allowed for it was small, and he was in great difficulty in finding the necessary ready money.

I further submit that my client has not breached the Army Act. The police went to his place and threatened to lock him up and told him he would have to clear out of the town, a most high-handed proceeding. I ask Your Worships to say something about that in your judgement. What right have the police to go there and insult the man? It is true that the Act said that a publican must provide accommodation, but when put to the practical test, it was very hard. Perhaps he had not the necessary money to find forage day by day and he was told that morning, incidentally, that a petition was being presented by the innkeepers to proper authorities in regard to the billet allowance for the horses. Every available stall of Mr Williams had been taken, and on market days a number of people usually put up at the Black Boy. If my client had lost trade through the military horses being in his stalls it was hard. My client keeps his house respectably although he was threatened that he would have to leave the town at once. I appeal to Your Worships to dismiss the case.

The defendant himself appeared in the witness box with a self-defence was based on his perception of unfairness. He explained in replies to Mr George:

Williams:	There are a number of public houses in the town with very large stables without any of the horses. There are about 104 horses come to the town and I have 42. I've complained to the sergeant major and to Sergeant Driscoll and to most of those in authority that I can't supply that number of animals without money. I had no complaint from Sergeant Ellson, and he was the sergeant in charge. As to the sergeant's suggestion that I had had a drop too much to drink, that is only his suggestion. I'm not a teetotaller but I don't often take a drop too much, and I don't think the police have ever seen me worse for drink in my house. And as well as the feed, I provided hay. It was the men's fault if they didn't use it. I would also like to say that as well as providing accommodation and forage, I have supplied them with paraffin oil, stable lamps, boxes, buckets, brooms, shovels, forks and other utensils. I bought 12 new buckets for their use, and I have to get up at 6.30 each day to let the men in.
Sgt Davies:	When Sgt-Major Morgan complained that there was not sufficient oats, what answer did you give?
Williams:	I can't tell you.
Sgt Davies:	Is it true he asked you to put in more oats?
Williams:	I believe he did. I was giving what I thought was correct. I did not say I would not give some, I said I thought it was sufficient. As to the straw, the men used clover instead. I had a ton of clover in a loft and they used it all.

This closed the defendant's evidence and Mr George remarked to the Bench that he would like them to know that as a result of the prosecution, the defendant had to leave the inn. This was rather hard as he had seven children. In his opinion, it was all a storm in a tea cup and he looked forward to the day when the war would be over and the defendant would have to rely on the civilian population instead of the military.[36] Here was another comment indicating the economic importance of the Welsh Horse being in town.

The magistrates did not see it George's way, however, and considered that the case had been made out very clearly.
The chairman said:

> 'The officer appointed to supervise the feeding of the horses pointed out that it was not satisfactory and asked the defendant to correct that, but he only replied with abusive language. If the animals were not properly fed by the person upon whom that duty devolved under the billeting regulations, the responsibility was his. The defendant had every opportunity to redress the complaint, and he having failed to do so there is only one course open to the Bench. The minimum penalty for the offence was £2 and the maximum £5. The defendant will be fined 50s. and costs.'[37]

Sydney Jarvis for Ind Coope and Company informed the Bench that the company had no sympathy at all with the conduct of the defendant, in consequence of which he would have to leave the house under the terms of the contract. They realised that it was a very serious matter to interfere with military arrangements and they wanted to do everything in their power to assist. Their local manager, Charles Hackett, had already taken over the billeting, and attention to the horses, and a new tenant was being sought.

---

[36] This comment reported in *The Montgomeryshire Express*, 19/1/1975.

[37] As a comparison, this amount was equivalent to six months' salary for the inspector of lodging houses. Powys County Archives, *Newtown Urban District Council minute book*, item no. M/UD/NL/15.

Conclusion

The arrival of the Welsh Horse Yeomanry in Newtown may well have been engineered by David Davies M.P. in an attempt to improve the financial situation of the town. Hundreds of men and animals entered the town meaning that a great deal of money was added to the local economy through the billeting of the force over the period of their stay. Their contribution to the social life of the depressed area would also have been very welcome. John Williams was probably thinking of income when he initially reported that he could accommodate 42 animals, but the burden of paying for the feed up front while having to wait for recompense from the government proved too much for him to be able to bear and he lost the tenancy through a prosecution for failing to provide proper feed. Williams had been tenant for no more that four years, as the 1911 census shows Charlotte Percival as licensee. Now he, his wife and seven children were out of their house and home. The Welsh Horse which had brought extra income for many in the town had actually brought disaster for this particular family.

Epilogue

In August 1916, notice was given that both the Welsh Horse Yeomanry and a contingency of the Royal Welsh Fusiliers were to be removed from Newtown and sent to Welshpool. Clerk to Newtown Urban District Council, Martin Woosnam, wrote to David Lloyd George who was Secretary of State for War, with an appeal against the removal. At a council meeting on 16 August 1916, Woosnam read out a reply from Lloyd George explaining the compromise that the Fusiliers would stay but the Yeomanry would go to Welshpool.[38] The council then offered a vote of thanks to Woosnam for his efforts.[39] The intimation is that the loss of both units would have been a great blow to Newtown.

---

[38] See minutes of Newtown Urban District Council, Powys County Archives, item ref. M/UD/NL/M15; *The Montgomeryshire Express*, 22/8/1916.

[39] Woosnam and Lloyd George were friends both politically and socially. The two had gone fishing together on the Severn at Llandinam on David Davies M.P.'s land. R Jones, Williams Scott Owen and Martin Woosnam: two Montgomeryshire

During their time in Newtown, two supplementary regiments of the Welsh Horse Yeomanry were formed. These new forces were relatively short lived and their men went on to join the reserve regiments of the Montgomeryshire Yeomanry with which they trained recruits. The original, Cardiff-formed regiment and the first-formed regiment of the Montgomeryshire Yeomanry, however, amalgamated and saw action in Gallipoli, Egypt, Palestine and, ultimately, the Western Front.[40] They were in active service when the armistice was declared,[41] and two of their number received the Victoria Cross for outstanding service.[42]

These regiments saw active service in a dismounted form, their horses having been commandeered for other service on the front.[43] In those roles the animals experienced the same terrible conditions as the men in the conflict that became known as The Great War.[44]

---

worthies', (2010), 98 *The Montgomeryshire Collections*, 96–7.

[40] Owen, *Roscomyl*, pp. 30-3. For detailed account of the Palestine campaign see Wynn, *The Historical Records*, pp. 59–100. Confusion can arise from the nomenclature used for army units as the word regiment was used in a different way for mounted ones, compared to foot soldiers. Up to September 1914 there was only one regiment known as the Welsh Horse. It was at that time ordered to create a duplicate which became the 2/1st regiment and later it created a third, known as the 3/1st regiment. The Welsh Horse was thus triplicated. Essentially, the 1/1st was the "overseas service" unit and the other two were 'reserve units'. The job of the reserves was to train recruits and eventually send them on to the 1/1st. It was the 1/1st that saw active service at the front. (Personal correspondence with Chris Baker, founder of the internet resource *The Long, Long Trail – the British Army in the Great War of 1914–1918* (http://www.1914–1918.net/).

[41] Bredsdorf, *Welshpool*, p. 145.

[42] Sgt John Collins, Welsh Horse Yeomanry; Sgt William Waring, Montgomeryshire Yeomanry. See Wynn, *The Historical Records*, pp. 152–5 for a full list of honours received by the regiments. For an excellent summary of the history of both the Montgomeryshire and Welsh Horse Yeomanries see www.1914–1918.net (viewed 6/11/2010).

[43] Wynn, *The Historical Records*, p. 69.

[44] See S. Butler, *The War Horses: The Tragic Fate of a Million Horses Sacrificed in the First World War* (Wellington, 2011).

THE WELSH LANGUAGE
SOME REFLECTIONS ON ITS HISTORY

The Right Honourable the Lord Judge PC

Hywel Dda Inaugural Lecture
University of Swansea

22 June 2011

> England, what have you done to make the speech
> My fathers used a stranger at my lips
> An offence to the ear, a shackle on the tongue
>
> R.S. Thomas, *The Old Language*, *ll.*1–3.[1]

THESE are the haunting words of R.S. Thomas, the poet of Aberdaron, a great poet lamenting that he could not express himself in his native language, Welsh. How could this be? How did this happen?

The answer to these questions would require scholarship of a depth which I do not have, and knowledge on a scale of which I am ignorant. But I offer some tentative thoughts on the subject, largely historical, conscious of the honour that has been done to me by the invitation to give this inaugural Hywel Dda Lecture.

Perhaps we should begin with Thomas Hobbes in the *Leviathan* that:

> The general use of Speech is to transfer our Mental Discourse, into Verbal; or Trayne of our Thoughts, into a Trayne of Words[2]

It is systems of words, commonly shared among the group, that identifies a tribe, or a community, or using modern language, a nation. We know that animals of the same kind communicate with each other, but it is only the human animal that turns the noises into distinguishable and consistent sounds. It was not until I became a grandfather that I appreciated the

---

[1] R.S. Thomas, *Collected Poems* (London, 1993), p. 25. The poem was originally published in the poet's second collection, *An Acre of Land*, in 1952.

[2] Thomas Hobbes, *Leviathan* (1651): Part One – Of Man; *Chapter IV* – Of Speech.

extraordinary facility of the human brain which put starkly comes to this. If the child in the cot or in his or her mother's arms hears mother or father speaking English, then the sounds which will eventually emerge will be the English language; if Swahili, then Swahili; if Mandarin, then Mandarin; if Welsh, then Welsh. As a father I think I took it for granted. As a grandfather it has struck me as utterly miraculous. The acquisition of this method of communication between human beings which we take for granted is indeed a miracle.

But this is not a lecture about miracles. But the starting point of a lecture on this type of topic needs to emphasise how crucial the issue of language is to the very survival of the human race. Therefore I could not have started nearer the beginning than the acquisition of language by a child. Nevertheless these miraculous processes underpinned the survival of Welsh.

Now I must move to a different starting point. Completely at random (as no doubt you will all believe) I pick 1244. During that year it was pointed out to the royal Justiciar visiting South Wales:

> It is not easy in our region to reward or restrain the Welsh, unless this is done by someone of their own tongue.

The inference is inescapable. What else was this recording except that 800 years ago the people of Wales were speaking Welsh and that the language of Wales was readily identifiable? It was the unique and thriving tongue in which these men and women expressed themselves. To put it into context, by now William the Marshal had already built his great castles at Chepstow, Newport, and Pembroke.

Right in the middle of the great castle building programme of Edward I, a few years later, we find a record in the Welsh Assize Roll of 1277-1284 which includes this poignant lament:

> All Christians have laws and customs in their own lands; even the Jews in England have laws among the English; we had our immutable laws and customs in our land until the English took them away after the last war.

.

I hope no one here will misunderstand me when I say that the reference to the Jews must have been entirely deliberate. In medieval Christian communities Jews were treated appallingly. So the reference to Jews was deliberate: what this meant was that we in Wales were being treated even worse than that. We have been robbed of our own law and customs, laws among others of Hywel Dda.

In the wake of the great castles of North Wales, there is one further significant feature to notice. Perhaps inevitably, it was not just castles. There was, in addition, settlement by what we should describe as colonists. It was not a coincidence that in 1284 charters were granted to a large number of towns, including Flint, Rhuddlan, Conwy, Caenarfon, Criccieth and Harlech, and in the calendar of ancient petitions we had a protest from the colonists:

> That so many Welsh are lodged near the town on the outside that they disturb the profit and market of the English.

That complaint came from Rhuddlan. So the castles themselves, intimidating though they were, were attracting communities of men and women from Wales, no doubt looking for work, and food, speaking their own established Welsh language.

But, and this is an important but, when we are looking back at medieval times, in the context of language, we must pause and understand the medieval world. At this date in England society was multi-lingual. French was still the language of the nobility and the aristocracy. Men spoke and on occasions wrote in French to demonstrate their high status and education. The language of the Court was French or Norman French. There had been no Shakespeare: no Authorised Version of the Bible; the concept of national identity in England was far from secure. What we can discern are trends.

In 1295 Edward I declared that it was the intention of the French intending to invade, to eliminate English, a piece of propaganda revived by his grandson Edward III. But what was English?

Despite its Latin title, *Cursor Mundi* was written in English in about 1300. It demanded that each country should have its own language. Plainly that would apply to Wales. In 1323 a defendant to a charge of theft, claiming to be a cleric, refused to answer save in English. He was asked if he knew how to speak in Latin or in French. He said that he was English, and English born. And therefore he would speak in his mother tongue and refused to speak anything but English. The end result was that he was treated as not entering any plea at all and visited with that ghastliness, *peine forte et dure*, in effect weighed down with stones until the breath was crushed out of him. This heroic martyr helps to underline that the issue of language is not some quirky product of a pressure group. It would matter, it does matter to men and women of every nation.

Next I come to a statute, this time written in French, but using its English title, the Pleadings in English Act of 1362.

This declared its purpose.

> (2) ...the said laws and customs the rather shall be perceived and known, and better understood in the tongue used in the said realm, and by so much every man of the said realm may the better govern himself without offending of the law, and better keep, save, and defend his heritage and possessions:[3]

And the remedy:

> (3) and in diverse regions and countries, where the King, the nobles, and others of the said realm have been, good governance and full right is done to every person, because that their laws and customs be learned and used in the tongue of that country.[4]

So there it was, statutory recognition in Parliament of the importance that the laws and usages of the community should be properly understood by the members of the community, and that the language used to enforce the laws and customs should be the language used by the member of the community itself. The ideal was noble. There was no great rush to enforce it in England, but English was developing at great speed, and the French and Latin and old Anglo-Saxon components were gradually moulding together. English was in Robert Burchfield's delectable phrase, a language of "amazing hospitality" – and so it remains, constantly developing, constantly taking new words in from all cultures, and at the same time establishing itself across the world. I shall return to this consideration at the end of the lecture.

---

[3] 36 Ed. 3, st. 1, c. 15.

[4] Ibid.

But again, going back to the fourteenth century, none of this was clear. Indeed for the "establishment" in England it can be argued that the use of the local or native language was regarded as something of a threat. For example, at the turn of the 14th and 15th centuries, it was declared that the sacrament of the Mass was not to be discussed in the vernacular, and as for the Bible in English, that did not come up for discussion, save in the sense that monks and scholars were allowed to use it if authorised. Wycliffe's Bible in English was not welcome. In England the language of dissent was English.

Throughout this period, Welsh, as far as I can see, continued to flourish. There was no reason why the language should not have continued to be used and to develop in Wales. According to Miri Rubin, even the English marcher lords "developed a great liking for the sounds and generic diversity of Welsh poetry; for the Welsh *cywyddau*… for the elegy or the ode". She quotes, and I do, Ieuan Llwyd ab Ieuan's elegy for his beloved wife, Angharad, on her death:

> A fitting pain, a shower of tears wets me,
> My cheek is sallow and withered by languishing grief;
> …sad work for the sight, the long enforced weeping;
> Woeful work of longing, the memory of Angharad.

The quotation is, as you have heard, in English. Someone will one day recite to me how it sounds in Welsh. A poem of haunting beauty, written long before the poetry of Wyatt or Howard or William Shakespeare, evidence that the language of Wales was thriving, and vivid, and perhaps in one word, communicative. And there was no reason why it should not have continued to thrive.

Until we come to the Tudors. The Tudors. A Welsh monarch on the throne. His son half Welsh. All should have been well.

The Laws in Wales Act of 1535, sometimes called the Act of Union, was the main provision directly connected with Wales enacted by the Reformation Parliament, one of the most momentous in our history.[5] It asserted that the "imperial crown" of England, "incorporated and united and annexed Wales" into the "Realm of England". In passing, note that the

[5] 27 Hen. 8, c. 26.

same language was used in the statute which was to govern religion, the Act in Restraint of Appeals a year or two earlier, which declared that "this England is an Empire". Henry VIII had some grand ideas – on the Continent foreigners tended to believe that all Englishmen had tails and were usually drunk.

Now to the justification, or explanation for the Laws in Wales Act:

> The People of the same Dominion have and do daily use a Speech nothing like, nor consonant to the natural Mother Tongue used within this Realm.

Of course, with typical Tudor hypocrisy, and you will gradually discern that I am not a great admirer of loveable, bluff, old Henry VIII with his six wives, it was true that Welsh was not a speech used in England. But it was used in Wales. There it was the natural Mother tongue. And so, having unified Wales to England, the statute went on to provide:

> That from henceforth no Person or Persons that use the Welsh Speech or Language shall have or enjoy any Manner Office or Fees within this Realm of England, Wales or other the King's dominions, upon pain of forfeiting the said office or fees, unless he or they use the English speech or tongue.

So either you spoke English, or you were excluded from public life in your own country, or any office, including judicial office: you would not advance in the world. Yet who in the end does not hope for some improvement in his life, for greater opportunities for his children? In Wales it all seemed to depend on the abandonment of the use of language which, if Welsh, you learn to articulate when your mother and father spoke to you when you were a baby.. It was an "outrage". That was the word I used in my own judgment in *Williams* v *Cowell* in July 1999.[6] To my mind it was made worse by the utter hypocrisy of the further statutory requirement that in courts in Wales, and contrary to the provisions of the 1362 Act, Welsh people were prohibited from using their own language. What had happened to the principle established nearly 200 years earlier in the 1362 Act?

The reality is that the later half of the reign of Henry VIII was filled with outrages. He was, after all, the Supreme Head of the Church, and believed

---

[6] [2000] 1 WLR 187 at 199.

himself to be God's lieutenant on Earth. And so, as with every tyrant, his personal wishes coincided with those of the Almighty. It is a shattering potion. The dissolution of the monasteries – not the reform of monasteries which were sick, or corrupt, or venal, or crammed with immorality – which had begun in Cardinal Wolsey's time – but the complete dissolution of centuries old places of worship, and assistance, and education, and learning was but one huge act of criminal damage. All that I am getting at is encapsulated in the exercise in terrorism which followed his personal promise – the King's personal promise – the promise of God's anointed - to Robert Aske that those who joined the Pilgrimage of Grace dispersed, would be pardoned, and he would hold Parliament at York with "free election of knights and burgesses" is summarised in his letter to the Duke of Norfolk:

> You shall, in any wise, call such dreadful execution to be done upon a good number of the inhabitants of every town, village, and hamlet, that have offended in this rebellion, as well as by the hanging of them up on tress as by the quartering of them... as they be a fearful spectacle of all other hereafter...it shall be much better that these traitors shall perish in their wilful, unkind, and traitorous follies, than that so slender punishment should be done upon them as the dread thereof should not be a warning to others...in the eye of their remembrance, might percase upon light rumours, tales, and suggestions of evil persons, fall into the pit of light mischief...

And not long afterwards the Statute of Proclamations enacted what we now, with disparagement, describe as Henry VIII clauses, granting powers to the King, in effect, without parliamentary approval. Rule by executive regulation: this remains a pernicious danger to the rule of law, and in recent years the habit has revived. We should be very watchful.

Wales was not alone in its suffering at the hands of this Tudor King. I do not offer these observations in order to imply that the Laws in Wales Act was less than an outrage. That is what it was. But it was one outrage, among a number of other outrages. And it is my belief that this single Act of Parliament, and its consequences, was ultimately more damaging to the language of Wales, and its use in Wales, than the more dramatic, attention seeking castles of the Plantagenet Kings.

To reinforce this thought, we should remember that this was a time of wide political and religious ferment. All over Europe the Bible was translated into the vernacular, with printing presses churning out numerous copies of it to be read by people familiar with their own language. In the reign of Elizabeth I, the right to read the Bible in English was firmly established, and no less important, she authorised the publication of the Bible in Welsh in 1588, to join the Welsh translation of the Prayer Book in the churches of Wales. Again, the inference is plain. In Wales, when the Laws in Wales Act 1535 was enacted, the Welsh language was in common use. Otherwise why provide for the Bible in Welsh? Doesn't this underline the hypocrisy of the 1535 Act.

The decision that the Bible should be published in Welsh was another crucial moment. It must have contributed, in communities where the Christian religion retained its vitality, to the very survival of the Welsh language. It is not cynical, but maybe perhaps it is, that on one view this meant that it was acceptable for Welsh speakers to accumulate their treasures in Heaven, provided they did nothing which might allow them to accumulate treasure on Earth.

And the impact, very gradually, of the first 1535 Act was the destruction of the Welsh language in large parts of the country. Perhaps "destruction" is not the right word. Perhaps it was an enervating process, gradual decline by desuetude. To speak Welsh was not the way forward to advancement. Nevertheless loyalty to the Welsh language continued. So, in 1830 the absorption of the legal system of Wales into that of England was completed when the Courts of Great Sessions of Wales were abolished altogether, and the old Assize system which had operated in England was now applied in Wales. But these courts had survived for 300 years after Henry VIII. And in 1846 the county courts in England and Wales were created, with a county court boundary system, which meant that some were entirely in Wales, and one spanned Wales and some of the English bordering counties. I think it significant that it was recognised that where possible judges who were acquainted with the Welsh language should be appointed to the county courts of Wales. It means, of course, that again it was recognised that in some parts of Wales, at any rate, the language continued in common use, and it also underlined that by the mid nineteenth century, at any rate, that whatever Henry VIII might have ordered, the

Welsh language had been and was inevitably going to be used in some areas of court business.

As Professor Gwynedd Parry demonstrates in his fascinating biography of Sir David Hughes Parry,[7] Caernarvonshire remained "a fortress and a bastion for the Welsh language". He supports his thesis by referring to the 1891 census figures which show that more than 65% of the population of Caernarfonshire spoke *only* Welsh, and only about 10% could not speak Welsh at all. Taking Wales as a whole, something like 30% could speak *only* Welsh. In the small rural parishes of North Wales, it is highly probable that the entire population spoke Welsh. What is consistent with the census figures is perhaps demonstrated by the Government Report on Education in Wales published in 1847. It speaks of:

> The mockery of an English trial of a Welsh criminal by a Welsh jury, addressed by counsel and judge in English.

It was

> too gross and shocking to need comment. It is nevertheless a mockery which must continue until the people are taught the English language…

In Victorian England, even early Victorian England, it does not appear to have occurred that the solution might be the repeal of the Laws in Wales Act. And that, in truth, is unsurprising. These were the years of Empire, not Henry VIII's empire, but the British Empire, to which in all its manifestations, good as well as bad – and there were many good manifestations – people from Wales made their own contributions. To this day there are still areas in Argentina where Welsh is spoken. However whatever may have been happening in Caernarvonshire, or for that matter in Argentina, in the South, in the Valleys, Welsh was in serious decline, and indeed it was declining in the North too. There were many factors.

This remarkable decline in the use of the Welsh language coincided with the extraordinary changes in social and industrial history of the nineteenth and early half of the last century, for example, the industrial revolution, the economic disasters of the '20s and '30s, two destructive World Wars, in

[7] R. Gwynedd Parry, *David Hughes Parry: A Jurist in Society* (Cardiff, 2010).

particular the First World War. There were more insidious changes. The use of Welsh by children in Wales was actively discouraged. By active I do not mean correction, but punishment: punishment not meted out only by teachers who were English but by teachers who were Welsh. And Welsh was not taught in schools. From now on survival depended entirely on parents speaking Welsh to their children. By the 1971 census, by contrast with 1891, the number of Welsh speakers throughout Wales was reduced to 20% of the population, so 80% did not speak the language at all, and even in what Dr Gwynedd Parry describes as the "solid heartlands", the figure was down to 60%. The language of Wales had gone from being a language of the majority to the language of the minority. That seems to me to be a sad story.

The result is summarised in a memorandum written by a prosecuting counsel in the trial of Saunders Lewis and two others in October 1936 for arson at an RAF school on the Lleyn Peninsula. He pointed out:

> The King's Commission is written only in English… no mention of Wales is made and in the entire ceremonial the existence of such a place as Wales is ignored.

The judge rejected the applications of three fluent Welsh speakers to address the court in Welsh. It is said that generally he was utterly contemptuous of them. The jury did not agree its verdicts. They were re-tried at the Old Bailey and convicted.

After the trial, a petition was launched at the Eisteddfod in Cardiff in August 1938. It had asserted that the statutes of Henry VIII were:

> A source of injustice and indignity to British subjects whose native language is Welsh…

The prayer of the petitioners was for an Act of Parliament that would place

> the Welsh language on a footing of equality with the English language in all proceedings connected with the administration of justice and of public services in Wales….

Mark these words.

As ever, the ghastliness of war produces some unanticipated results. The Nazi conquest of Europe brought many refugees to our shores – resistance fighters from Holland and Norway and France among them. Arrangements were made for these individuals to be tried, when charged, in courts in which their own language was used. Yet this was not then available in Wales. Then in October 1942, the Welsh Courts Act 1942 repealed the language clause in the Laws in Wales Act 1535. One of my predecessors, Lord Caldecote, commented in April 1943 that Welsh was:

> …a foreign language to me and, to tell you the truth, I do not know that I feel very sympathetic to this plan for keeping alive, what, like Erse and Gaelic, is really a dying language.

I do not think that the fact that bombs were falling in London provides any excuse: but it demonstrates that it took a huge amount of energy, and a vast amount of commitment, and dedication, and determination to halt the decline of the use of Welsh, and now to ensure its revival.

The 1942 Act did not treat Welsh as equal with English. It permitted the use of Welsh to a party or witness who believed that he would be at a disadvantage if forced to use English when his natural language of communication was Welsh. Nevertheless, even in Wales, not everyone agreed with this measure. For example, the Associated Law Society of Wales protested that such a measure was brought forward "in time of war". But enacted it was.

It was in the context of subsidiary legislation prescribing forms of oaths in Welsh that this enactment was considered in *The Queen* v *Merthyr Tydfil Justices* ex parte *Jenkins*[8] when the Divisional Court considered the case of a schoolmaster, fluent in English, charged with driving without a licence, who asserted that he would not plead to the charges until they were put to him in the Welsh language. Pleas of "not guilty" were entered. He then sought to cross-examine a police witness in Welsh, and was not allowed to do so. When he gave evidence he was allowed to give it in Welsh. He was convicted. He relied on section 1 of the 1942 Act and asked for his convictions to be quashed because he had been denied his rights.

[8] [1967] 1 All ER 636.

It did not help before the Divisional Court that it was conceded on his behalf – as it had to be – that he had no defence to the charges. That is an unpromising foundation for a successful appeal. From his observations it is clear that Lord Parker, Chief Justice was not unsympathetic, but given the absence of any defence, the appeal could not be allowed. A Welsh judge, Mr Justice Glynn Jones took the same view. Mr Justice Widgery, another of my predecessors, expounded his view in the context of his experience of having spent the summer on circuit in Wales.

> It is quite clear that the proper language for the court proceedings in Wales is the English language.

The use of Welsh impeded:

> The efficient administration of justice in Wales.

He went on to describe the very limited rights given by the 1942 Act, and concluded that

> language difficulties which arise in Wales can be dealt with by discretionary arrangements for an interpreter, precisely in the same way as language difficulties at the Central Criminal Court are dealt with when the accused is a Pole.

So the 1942 Act had not delivered the official recognition for Welsh sought by many leading figures – but – as I have underlined – not by all influential figures in Welsh public life.

In *Evans* v *Thomas,*[9] a completed nomination paper for a candidate for election as a county councillor was completed in Welsh, and rejected by the county returning officer on that ground. It was not "in the prescribed form as laid down by statute". The only other candidate was therefore elected. The petition was for that election to be declared void. Everyone involved understood and read Welsh, including the claimant, the elected candidate, and the returning officer.

The Divisional Court decided that the 1942 Act had not authorised the use of the Welsh language in a nomination paper: "It is desirable" said

[9] [1962] 3 All ER 108.

Winn LJ, "that it should be clearly appreciated that the court is no more concerned… with any general question of the status of Welsh as a national language than it is to animadvert on the reasons or emotions which inspired the petitioners' refusal to employ English in their nomination paper".

It is not difficult to understand why those who were campaigning for Welsh to be treated on the basis of equality were disappointed with the Act. It is only fair to the judges in these cases to indicate that a proper statutory interpretation of the Act left them with no choice. The alternative construction was not realistically available. But, even looking back to what is now the not so distant past, is it perhaps too much to have asked for at least a level of understanding of the issues, a little less sense of disparagement in the disposal of the argument? Indeed Sir David Hughes Parry was driven to dismiss Widgery J's remarks as language which can "be fairly interpreted by lay men to carry a biased, Anglo-Saxon nineteenth century political flavour". In short, the future Lord Chief Justice was given a "wigging".

And so we come to the Welsh Language Act 1967. Perhaps we should pause for a minute. There was a new judicial understanding afoot, exemplified in the quashing by the Court of Appeal of a sentence of three months' imprisonment imposed on students from Aberystwyth who disrupted a very high profile defamation trial to register a protest in support of the Welsh language. The trial judge sent them to prison for three months. Within a week their appeal was allowed. They were released and bound over to keep the peace and to be of good behaviour. At the time of this demonstration, I had recently been called to the Bar, and I remember the case very well. It was indeed one of those demonstrations that really matter, perhaps because the tide of history was flowing in the right direction. Notwithstanding their clear and deliberate contempt of court, Lord Denning and his colleagues were not unsympathetic.

Lord Denning pointed out:

> These young people are no ordinary criminals. There is no violence, dishonesty or vice in them. On the contrary, there was much that we should applaud. They wish to do all they can to preserve the Welsh language. Well may they be proud of it. It is the language of the Bards –

> of the poets and the singers – more melodious by far than our rough English tongue.[10]

Professor Parry points out that perhaps Lord Denning was drawing on his own experiences as a young officer attached to the 38th Welsh Division in France in 1918, when he was shoulder to shoulder with Welsh soldiers digging trenches under continuous shell fire. At some stage in that ghastly conflict we should perhaps remember that Lord Denning himself, then of course a much younger man than we remember him now, had been awarded the Military Cross for his personal bravery in battle.

The Welsh Language Act 1967 expanded the use of the Welsh language in courts by permitting any party or witness or other person "who desires to use it" to do so. It was no longer necessary to demonstrate need, or disadvantage, or difficulty with the use of English. The individual could choose for himself or herself. It was not what we may describe nowadays as the "full Monty" and in particular did not fully implement the principle of total equality between English and Welsh in courts in Wales. And it was not directed to wider aspects of public life. But, and this is an important but, perhaps at the time it was as far as it could realistically go. When considering an Act of Parliament, realism includes political realities, and it must be acknowledged that there were many Welsh men and women living in Wales who did not share the zeal for the Welsh language which enthused, for example, the students from Aberystwyth.

And finally for the present, we come to the Welsh Language Act 1993. This proclaims the principle that:

> In the conduct of public business and the administration of justice in Wales the English and Welsh languages should be treated on the basis of equality…

The principle is clear and simple. The trumpet has sounded. The "outrage" of the 1535 Act has at long last, been eradicated. All this was confirmed in the Government of Wales Act 1998, which created the National Assembly for Wales and underlined the principle that so far as "both appropriate in

---

[10] *Morris* v *Crown Office* [1970] 2 QB 114.

the circumstances and reasonably practicable", the English and Welsh languages should be treated "on a basis of equality".

The petition launched in Cardiff in August 1938 has been answered. At last. I have said before, and I repeat, that the judiciary applies this principle of equality. In a court in Wales, if the litigant, or the witness, wishes to use the Welsh language, then he or she has an absolute right to do so: it is not a discretion vested in the judge, it is an entitlement vested in the citizen. All documents relating to processes in court are available in both languages. No less than 49 of our judges in Wales are fluent Welsh speakers: so are 350 magistrates. And there will be more.

Of course, this is not the end of the story. As a judge I have no better insight into the future than anyone else, and moreover, as a judge I shall not make observations about what can truly be described as political issues. The way in which Welsh will be used in this country, and I do not merely mean its official status, but encompass its actual use in day to day transactions and for communications between citizens of Wales, is a political and social question. But for the foreseeable future, I believe that the survival of the Welsh language is assured.

But there is corollary to the truism that the future is uncertain, that "what's to come is still unsure", and that is that you cannot foretell the future. So we must pause at the moment of assurance and remind ourselves that Welsh must survive in an international environment in which English is, if not the dominant language, certainly one of the dominant languages of the world, and likely to remain so. In a world of new and extraordinary methods of communication that is a consideration which should not be overlooked. I do most earnestly hope that the figures I gave you at the beginning do not presage impact on this new world.

How do I end this quick dash through 800 years of history? The thoughts are very simple. The language of Wales is a precious heritage. It has survived. But there is no room for relaxed smugness. Its survival is thanks to a relatively small number of people who for centuries stood by it, probably against their own economic and social self-interest. When I visit Aberdaron, as I frequently do when on holiday in North Wales, I offer a metaphorical little bow to R.S. Thomas. If the language his fathers used were ever again to become a stranger at his lips, or an offence to the ear, or a shackle on the tongue, all the effort and sacrifice would have been in vain. But never take the future for granted. Speaking as Lord Chief Justice of Wales, I can only urge you to safeguard your language. Guard it well.

JURISDICTION AND JUDICIAL AUTHORITY[1]

The View from Wales

Thomas Glyn Watkin

Laws for Wales

ON 4 May 1881, Edward Warton, the Conservative Member of Parliament for Bridport, rose to address the House of Commons on the Second Reading of a Bill. The Bill was the Sunday Closing (Wales) Bill, which had as its intention the prohibition of the sale of alcoholic drinks on licensed premised in Wales on Sundays. A bill to the same purpose had failed for lack of parliamentary time the previous year. It seemed destined for greater success on this second occasion.[2]

One is tempted to admire Warton's courage – or at least his sense of purpose – in rising to address an audience composed in the main of men of a different stamp to himself, for – as references in the speeches make clear – most of members present were Liberal MPs sitting for Welsh constituencies who supported the bill. Warton made it clear that his opposition was not grounded solely on his objections to depriving those who wanted a drink on Sundays from having one in Wales; he was opposed to the whole notion of Parliament legislating for Wales apart from England. The thrust of his argument was that England and Wales was a single legal unit and Parliament should not contemplate legislating for one but not the other. England and Wales was for legal purposes a single territorial unit served by a single set of courts, and therefore it was not possible, he argued, for Wales to have separate laws of its own.

Whatever the scorn poured upon his views by those whom he opposed, his fire drew the Prime Minister, Gladstone, himself to the chamber to respond and muster support for the measure. Despite the ferocity – or perhaps because of the intemperance – of Warton's opposition the bill

[1] The text of a lecture delivered by the author at the Twenty-First British Legal History Conference, held at Glasgow University in July 2013.

[2] Parl. Deb. (Series 3) vol. 260 (1881) HC. The debates on the earlier bill can be found in vol. 253 (1880) HC.

obtained its second reading with a majority of 146 and, after further stringent attempts to block it in Committee and at the Third Reading, passed into law later that year.

The Sunday Closing (Wales) Act 1881 is generally regarded as being the first modern piece of legislation which applied only to Wales. It is seen as the precedent which paved the way for the passage of the Welsh Intermediate Education Act later that decade and perhaps, most significantly, for the Welsh Church Acts which subsequently disestablished the Church of England in Wales. It certainly established the principle that parliament could indeed make laws for Wales which were different from the laws in force in England.

Courts for Wales

Edward Warton's argument was that Wales could not have its own laws because it did not have a distinct legal system from that of England, in the sense of its own courts of law. Although his argument did not succeed, it raised sufficient concerns for quite a number of lawyers and judges from Wales to question whether Wales ought not to have its own law courts restored to it – namely the courts of Great Session created by the Tudors in the 1540s but abolished in 1830. Forty years after the passing of the Sunday Closing Act, with the principle that Wales could have its own laws firmly established, and with David Lloyd George as Prime Minister – albeit of a coalition government – the question of a separate system of courts came to be considered formally.

In the wake of the First World War, and with the imminent partition of Ireland requiring that legislative and judicial provision be made for Northern Ireland, a Conference on Devolution was established under the aegis of the Speaker, the Right Hon. Sir James Lowther MP, and that Conference in turn established a sub-committee under Lord Stuart of Wortley to consider whether separate judicial systems ought not to exist for England and for Wales, in the same manner as existed for Scotland and were about to come into being for Northern Ireland.

Strong views were expressed on the issue on both sides of the debate. Almost a century on, it is difficult not to be surprised at how strongly certain sections of the bar and also the bench in Wales supported the idea, with not only a hankering after a return of courts along the lines of the

Great Sessions but also of an appeals structure based on the Court of Exchequer Chamber rather than the contemporary Court of Appeal. Very much against the idea however were some of the senior civil servants working in the Lord Chancellor's Office, including the permanent secretary, Sir Claud Schuster.[3] In his evidence to the Speaker's Conference sub-committee, Schuster argued that Wales could not have its own law courts because it did not have its own laws, a key factor distinguishing it from both Scotland and Northern Ireland.[4] In its draft report, the sub-committee appeared to accept this essential link between a separate body of law and distinct judicial arrangements, for it suggested that the question of whether Wales should have its own law courts was essentially one for a Welsh legislature to determine if and when one ever came into existence. From the perspective of the 1920s, that can best be described as a pretty formidable kick for touch, although the committee's view that Wales should be given its own courts whenever a Welsh legislature decided that it should have them, and that any future devolution statute should embody that principle, is still quite a remarkable constitutional statement.[5]

---

[3] It is probably worth remembering that the Lord Chancellor in Lloyd George's coalition government was the man who had been amongst the most vehement opponents of the disestablishment of the Church in Wales a few years earlier, F.E. Smith, Lord Birkenhead.

[4] Schuster repeated his views in 1944 when a request was made for the appointment of a Secretary of State for Wales: see the letter from Sir Claud Schuster to Sir Alan Barlow (18/5/44): 'the Scottish and English judicial systems are, except for the appeal to the House of Lords, wholly distinct and separate, and operate a separate jurisprudence founded on different principles with different origins. The English and Welsh system of jurisprudence is a uniform integral whole operating a system of jurisprudence which is uniform, and has regard to the same principles, and springs from the same origins. The substantive law of England and Wales is not similar but the same, except for some minor immaterial differences.' National Archives, LCO 2/3214.

[5] "the only competent judge of the strength and purpose of the Welsh desires for separate judicial arrangements from those of England would, in our opinion, be a Welsh legislature or other legislative authority specially constituted under a scheme of Devolution to represent the people of Wales". National Archives, LCO 2/507, Draft Report, ¶ 11.

"we think that the creation of a Welsh judiciary should be effected if and when the Welsh legislature shall ask for it. It, if so desired, should be a Judiciary equal in

Constitutional statements aside, a comparison of the opposition arguments in the 1880s and 1920s is also worthy of remark, and it is to that comparison that I wish to draw attention in this paper. In 1881, it was argued that Wales could not have its own laws because it did not have its own courts. In 1920 it was argued that Wales could not have its own courts because it did not have its own laws. The circularity is amusing, but less so if capable of being concealed by a terminological subtlety, for a territory which has its own law courts can be described as a jurisdiction and likewise a territory which has its own laws. It has therefore been possible to say that Wales could not have its own laws because it was not a jurisdiction, and that it could not have its own courts because it was not a jurisdiction, thus concealing the circularity of the reasoning and giving the appearance of consistency. Frequently, the contrast with Scotland would be made because Scotland had its own laws and could therefore have its own courts, and having its own courts could have its own separate laws.

A Secretary of State for Wales

Over the following forty years, the contrast with Scotland was to be made repeatedly by ministers and civil servants in London when faced with requests for the creation of an office of Secretary of State for Wales on the lines of the post which had been created for Scotland in 1885. The creation of the Scottish Office in 1934 led to this issue being raised but with little success. Successive Prime Ministers – Neville Chamberlain before, Winston Churchill during and Clement Attlee after the Second World War – all declined to create such an office, often citing among their reasons the fact that, unlike Scotland, Wales was not a jurisdiction with its own laws and courts.[6] The reasons given frequently mirrored the arguments of the

---

independence to that of Scotland, with no appeal save to the House of Lords or its successor as the Supreme Appellate tribunal of the United Kingdom"; National Archives, LCO 2/507, Draft Report, ¶ 22.

[6] See the letter from Neville Chamberlain to Morgan Jones MP (27/7/1938): "The analogy of Scotland has been advanced... I think, however, that it must be recognised that the two cases are not parallel. For Scotland has always had different systems of law and administration from those in force in England... Wales, on the other hand, since Henry VII's (*sic*) Act of 1535, has been closely incorporated with England and there has not been, and is not now, any distinct law

opponents of Wales-only legislation in the 1880s, and ultimately met the same fate, for, despite the supposed difficulty, the office of Secretary of State for Wales was eventually created by the incoming Labour government of Harold Wilson in 1964.

The creation of the post of Secretary of State for Wales together with a government department, the Welsh Office, began the process of devolving executive functions and subordinate law-making powers to the Welsh Secretary from other government departments, such as health, education and housing. The functions so transferred formed the basis of the legislative competence given the National Assembly for Wales to pass subordinate legislation upon its creation in 1999[7] as well as its capacity to request primary law-making powers under the devolution settlement which existed between 2007 and 2011.[8] Indeed, those executive functions are still the historical foundation for the subjects over which the Assembly now enjoys fuller legislative powers following the referendum on primary law-making

---

or administrative system calling for the attention of a separate Minister.": NLW, *James Griffiths Papers*, C2/1. Also the letter from Winston Churchill to Megan Lloyd George MP (2/1/1945): "Thank you for your letter of November 10 regarding the proposals of the Welsh Parliamentary Party for the establishment of a Secretary of State for Wales. The matter is, as you know, receiving consideration. The difficulty is that a proposal of this nature has such far reaching implications in the administrative sphere that detailed consideration has to be given it by the many authorities concerned. These authorities are of course heavily burdened with war tasks.": NLW, *James Griffiths Papers*, C2/5. Also the following extract from the minutes of a meeting between the Lord President (Herbert Morrison MP), in company with other Ministers (Aneurin Bevan; Viscount Hall & James Griffiths) with a deputation of the Welsh Parliamentary Labour Group and of the Welsh Regional Council of Labour at 11, Downing Street on Friday, October 29th at 11.45am: "The Government were agreed that a Council for Wales and Monmouthshire would be useful, but they were opposed to the appointment of a Secretary of State for Wales, and they thought that to appoint a Minister of Cabinet rank to take the Chair at meetings of a Council for Wales would be open to something like the same objections. The real objection was that a Minister for Welsh Affairs, such as the Conservative Party had accepted at their Llandudno Conference, could only duplicate the work of Departmental Ministers. It was for the Departmental Minister concerned to handle Welsh requirements according to subject." NLW, *James Griffiths Papers*, C2/15.

[7] Under the Government of Wales Act 1998.

[8] Under the Government of Wales Act 2006, Part 3 and Schedule 5.

powers which took place in 2011.[9] Nevertheless, the Welsh Assembly's legislative competence still falls well short of the law-making powers of the Scottish Parliament, and a principal reason pleaded for denying the same level of competence to the Welsh Assembly as that given to the Scottish Parliament continues to be that, unlike Scotland, Wales does not have its own laws and law courts. Although Wales now has its own legislature and executive government, which between them are creating a body of law for Wales distinct to that which operates in England in the devolved areas, it is still not to be regarded a separate jurisdiction. Not surprisingly, both the National Assembly and the Welsh Government have interested themselves in the question of what therefore constitutes a jurisdiction,[10] and it is both interesting and informative the inquire into the manner in which the word is being used and has been sued in English over the centuries.

The Use of the word *Jurisdiction*

The *Oxford English Dictionary* gives four meanings for the word, *jurisdiction*, one of which is a metaphorical use of the word in non-legal contexts, but the other three of which are pertinent to these inquiries. These three meanings are:

- Administration of justice; exercise of judicial authority, or of the functions of a judge or legal tribunal; power of declaring and administering law or justice; legal authority or power. (1267; 1380; **1386**))
- The extent or range of judicial or administrative power; the territory over which such power extends. (1380; 1474; **1555**)
- A judicial organization; a judicature; a court, or series of courts, of justice. (**1765**)

These three meanings might be characterized as:

[9] Under the Government of Wales Act 2006, Part 4 and Schedule 7.

[10] See *National Assembly for Wales: Constitutional and Legislative Affairs Committee: Inquiry into the establishment of a separate Welsh jurisdiction* – December 2011; *Consultation responses* – March 2012; *Report* – December 2012; and *Welsh Government: Consultation Document: A Separate Legal Jurisdiction for Wales* – Number WG-15109 (27 March 2012).

- Jurisdiction as the activity or function of a court;
- Jurisdiction as the area or territory over which or within which that function is performed, and
- Jurisdiction as the manner in which the courts are organized in order to carry out that function.

The meanings are interrelated, but the first recorded use of the word with each of those meanings according to the *OED* reveals that each comes from a quite distinct historical period.

The first meaning, *jurisdiction* as the function of a court, the exercise of judicial authority, is traced by the *OED* to the Statute of Marlborough, 1267, although the word in the statute is the Latin *jurisdictio*. Although the wording of the statute is in Latin, the original meaning of a word in English is evidenced. This meaning is further evidenced by the provisions of the Statute of Gloucester a little over a decade later in 1278. The context is the separation of the cases which may be heard by the king's justices (the common law courts) from those which should be dealt with by the sheriff (the shire court). Those which were heard by the king's justices were to be heard according to the common custom of the realm (the emerging common law of England), while those heard by the sheriff would be adjudicated according to the custom of the shire. The distinction therefore was one of which body of law to apply, and the jurisdiction of the different courts was the exercise of the power to apply that body of law. By the end of the fourteenth century, this meaning had become the meaning of a word in English, where it is used of the several jurisdictions then existing in England, each served by a court or courts administering a distinct body of law. These included:

- the common law of the king's courts;
- the 'equity' (as it would later be called) of the Chancellor's court;
- the canon law of the ecclesiastical courts;
- the local customs of the shire, hundred and manorial courts;

- the international commercial law of the Admiral's court – which could be chosen by the merchants;[11]
- the commercial rules of the courts which regulated individual markets and fairs.

Not all of these jurisdictions were primarily territorial; some related to the status of persons, the performance of an activity or the existence of a relationship. For instance, the ecclesiastical courts claimed jurisdiction over all baptized persons, feudal courts over their lords' tenants and the king's courts over his free subjects.

This earliest English meaning of *jurisdiction* continues to be used today and is arguably the root meaning of the word, 'the power to declare and apply the law', in other words judicial authority. Jurisdiction in this sense is a function or activity, and the word need not be preceded by either the definite or indefinite article. A court has jurisdiction, indeed must have jurisdiction, and for any law to operate, there must be a person or body with the authority to administer it. One cannot sensibly have law without the power to administer it; one cannot sensibly have a power to administer it without a law to administer.

It is interesting to note that this is the meaning given to *jurisdiction* in what may be the only statute to date which has terminated within Wales the jurisdiction of courts previously exercising jurisdiction throughout England and Wales. Section 3(1) of the Welsh Church Act 1914 provides:

> As from the date of disestablishment ecclesiastical courts and persons in Wales and Monmouthshire shall cease to exercise any jurisdiction, and the ecclesiastical law of the Church in Wales shall cease to exist as law.[12]

---

[11] The three main customs employed were those of Barcelona, Oléron and Wisby which usually – but not necessarily – dealt respectively with trade in the Mediterranean, along the Atlantic seaboard and in the Baltic.

[12] The meaning of the last limb might be more clearly expressed today as 'the ecclesiastical law of the Church shall cease to exist as law in Wales', the Church being the Church of England and the title Church in Wales not having become the name of an institution at the time of the passing of the Act. It is also worth noting that the meaning of *Wales* in this context differs from both the meaning given in the Interpretation Act 1978 and that in the Government of Wales Act 2006.

Jurisdiction in this statute is something which is exercised, that is a power or function, and that is treated separately from the territory within which it is exercised (Wales and Monmouthshire) and the judicial system which exercises it (ecclesiastical courts and persons). Moreover, the provision makes the essential link between a body of law and jurisdiction, for the termination of jurisdiction also ended the existence of ecclesiastical law in Wales.[13]

The essential element of jurisdiction may therefore be said to be the existence of a body of law which needs to be administered. The power to administer law is the essence of jurisdiction.

The territorial dimension to the meaning of jurisdiction, on the other hand, is, according to the *OED*, first recorded in written English towards the end of the fourteenth century and during the fifteenth century, but always in relation to the jurisdiction of ecclesiastical persons. Its first recorded usage in a secular context comes from the middle years of the sixteenth century, which is significant as this is the time when Henry VIII was seeking to consolidate his political power within his realm. In England this involved the king asserting authority over the Church within his realm, so that the ecclesiastical jurisdiction became a further royal jurisdiction, and also by incorporating Wales and the Marches within the jurisdiction of the common law courts. Although the several jurisdictions of the common law, the Chancery and the ecclesiastical courts remained separate – as they would until the reforms of the nineteenth century, all were now courts with an authority coterminous with that of the kingdom.

In so far as the jurisdictions of these several royal courts remained separate, it would be difficult, indeed anachronistic, to describe them as a judicial system in the singular. It was the reform of the legal system during the 1870s which achieved this. The Judicature Acts of 1873–75 abolished the courts of common law, the Chancery, the Admiral's court and the recently-created Probate and Divorce Courts,[14] and transferred their jurisdictions, without amalgamation, to the new Supreme Court of

[13] The use of the word *jurisdiction* in its original sense can also be seen in the relevant provisions of the Government of Ireland Act 1920.

[14] These had been created in 1857 when jurisdiction over probate and matrimonial causes was removed from the ecclesiastical courts.

Judicature.[15] England and Wales had, for the first time, a unified judicial system. It was a jurisdiction in the third, organizational meaning of the term.

The first use of the word with this latest meaning is recorded by the *OED* as being in 1765, in the first volume of Blackstone's *Commentaries on the Laws of England* published in that year. That this usage should emerge at that time is significant, given that this was an age which saw a number of developments geared to centralizing and systematizing governmental authority in what began as the separate kingdoms of England, Scotland and Ireland, and ended as the United Kingdom, having passed through the stage of being Great Britain. It saw:

- the abolition of a separate Scottish parliament – 1707 (Great Britain created);
- the House of Lords asserting power to review decisions of the Court of Session in civil matters;
- the King's Bench asserting concomitant jurisdiction with the Great Sessions in Wales;
- the abolition of the differing inheritance customs of the provinces of Canterbury and York and the City of London;
- attempts to govern the American Colonies from the mother country leading to armed revolt;
- the existence of the Great Sessions subjected to attack;
- regular bills to reform the Court of Session – sometimes on the model of the English common law courts;
- the abolition of a separate Irish parliament – 1800 (the United Kingdom created).

Words do not acquire their meanings in a vacuum, but rather through use to express the perspective of the age in which or the person by whom they are being used. The English word *jurisdiction* acquired its connection with territory in the period when political and legal authority became synonymous with nation states, and acquired its connection with judicial organization and system in an age which emphasized the centralization and

[15] Now renamed the Senior Courts of England and Wales due to the creation of a Supreme Court of the United Kingdom.

unification of such authority within a ruler's territories. In England and Wales, this culminated in the judicial reforms of the 1870s. The effect of those reforms on the English concept of jurisdiction requires consideration.

The Meaning of Jurisdiction

The word *jurisdiction* is used less strictly in English than equivalent terms in other European languages – at least in doctrinal legal writings in those languages. It is this looser English usage which has enabled the concept to be used as a reason, or as an excuse, to block or attempt to block distinct legal provision for Wales (1880–1), giving Wales its own law courts (1920) or creating an office of Secretary of State for Wales (late 1930s/40s).

In juristic writing in several European countries, the word *jurisdiction* is strictly used to describe the authority of a court in doing what courts are established to do, namely administer a body of law regarding a particular legal subject. Wherever a body of law exists, there must be a court or courts with the authority to administer it, in the sense of stating it, applying it and, when necessary, interpreting it, in individual cases. This concept of *jurisdiction* refers to the authority of a court or courts to declare and apply a particular body of law, the first and earliest of the meanings attributed to the word *jurisdiction* in English by the *OED*. Thus, where there is a distinct body of criminal law, it follows that there must be courts charged with applying that law to particular cases – courts with criminal jurisdiction; where there is a distinct body of commercial law dealing with mercantile matters, there will have to be courts with the authority to declare and apply that body of law – courts with commercial jurisdiction. Wherever a distinct body of law exists, there has to be a court or courts with authority to declare and administer it – that is, with jurisdiction over it. *Jurisdiction* in this sense is a necessary concomitant of the existence of a distinct body of law. One cannot have one without the other. This remains true even when a court has jurisdiction over more than one body of law.

If therefore there is a separate body of law relating to Wales, it follows that there must be courts with jurisdiction to administer it. The existence of such a jurisdiction is a matter of fact not of choice. The choice relates to what is done in recognition of that fact. Viewed thus – *jurisdiction* as a sphere of activity, as authority over a particular body of law – the question relating to the legal status of Wales is not whether there *ought to be* or *can be* a Welsh jurisdiction but whether there *is* a Welsh jurisdiction and which courts exercise it.

The Loss of that Meaning

A strict distinction is also made in civil law countries between the jurisdiction of a court and its competence. Whereas the jurisdiction of a court relates solely to the question of what body or bodies of law it administers, its competence relates to three things: the territory within which it may exercise its jurisdiction, the subject-matter regarding which it may exercise its jurisdiction, and the level of adjudication which it is entitled to perform. Thus, for instance, a magistrates court with criminal jurisdiction may only be competent to hear and determine cases arising within its own locality, have a subject-matter competence limited to minor offences and will only be entitled to hear cases which are being tried for the first time – competence at first-instance.

In English, the term *jurisdiction* is sometimes used where a civil lawyer would use the term competence. There is therefore in English a danger of confusion between the two concepts of *jurisdiction* and *competence*. The nineteenth-century reforms of the judicial system may bear some responsibility for this possible confusion, for prior to those reforms, the English legal system knew of courts with separate jurisdictions over common law, equity, matrimonial causes, probate and Admiralty matters. After those reforms, the newly-created Supreme Court had jurisdiction over all of those bodies of law, the administration of which became fused in the new courts. Despite the oft repeated dogma that it was only the administration of those distinct bodies of law that was fused by the Judicature Acts not the bodies of law themselves, somewhat inevitably the unification of the courts has led to the various bodies of law which they administer also being viewed as a unity. The distinction between civil and criminal jurisdiction is the only serious survivor of the reform, if one leaves aside specialist tribunals such as the ecclesiastical courts.

The position of the ecclesiastical courts is however interesting, for, as has been noted, they have no jurisdiction in Wales as ecclesiastical law no longer exists there. If one postulates therefore that there is one body of law, the law of England and Wales, one is faced with the difficulty that one part of that law is only law in England and it is only in England that there are courts to administer it. Although the administration of ecclesiastical law has not been fused with that of common law and equity in what are now the Senior Courts, yet those courts do take judicial notice of its provisions and will act in aid of the ecclesiastical jurisdiction. Much of this ecclesiastical law is contained in Church of England Measures which become law on receiving royal assent following affirmative resolution in both Houses of Parliament. Such measures only make law for the provinces of Canterbury and York, which territory is more or less coterminous with the boundaries of England, but in so doing can and do amend laws which are laws of England and Wales, resulting in a change to those laws in England but leaving the law in Wales unaltered.[16] Insofar therefore as the Senior Courts administer those laws, they are called upon to administer a different law for England from that which they administer for Wales. Some provisions of the civil law relating to marriages fall within this category, and the Marriage Act 1949 recognizes this by listing such provisions in that Act in a Schedule headed 'Provisions of Statute which do not Extend to Wales'.

Although the Church of England has the competence to legislate, with Parliamentary approval, for England only, creating law which does not extend to Wales, the Welsh Assembly's Acts are deemed to extend to both England and Wales. The reason given for this is that there is only one legal system – that of England and Wales – and therefore although some laws may only apply to Wales or only apply to England, all such laws must extend to England and Wales. It is said with authority that 'there is no such thing as the law of England or the law of Wales; there is a single jurisdiction governed by the law of England and Wales... A proposition that a provision extends to Wales is therefore meaningless'.[17]

The Significance of that Loss

The meaning of 'a single jurisdiction' in that statement refers to there being but one set of courts, a single judicial organization. The reality is that the one set of courts is responsible for the administration of several bodies of law, that is it exercises several distinct jurisdictions. Once one recognizes that there are now some laws which apply only in England and some laws

[16] Recent examples are the Church of England Marriage Measure 2008 and the Church of England Marriage (Amendment) Measure 2012.

[17] *Craies on Legislation,* 8th ed., by Daniel Greenberg (London, 2004), p. 401.

which apply only in Wales, as well as laws which apply in both countries, and that it has not been doubted for almost a century that ecclesiastical laws which apply only in England are deemed only to extend to England as well, there is absolutely no reason why other laws which apply only to England or which apply only to Wales should not be treated similarly with regard to their extent. The current dogma that there can only be one law of England and Wales because England and Wales is 'a single jurisdiction' is founded on the concept of jurisdiction as judicial organization and a confusion of the concepts of jurisdiction and competence in the civilian sense of the terms. Once one pays due regard to the history of the term in English – and in English law, the need for the jurisprudential metaphysics of the distinction between *extent* and *applicability* in the current devolution settlement is at an end. One has only to recognize that there now exists a body of law which applies only in relation to Wales and decide which courts should administer that law. Those are the courts which should have jurisdiction. Questions as to whether they need to be different courts to those with jurisdiction over laws which apply only in England and/or which apply to both England and Wales become questions to be settled politically according to constitutional and practical considerations. A due regard for the past can inform the present and set a true direction for the future.

THE DEVELOPMENT BY ATTORNEY GENERALS OF THE DOCTRINE OF ARMED INTERVENTION BY STATES, WITHOUT SECURITY COUNCIL AUTHORISATION TO AVERT AN OVERWHELMING HUMANITARIAN CATASTROPHE

The Right Honourable the Lord Morris of Aberavon, KG, QC

The 2011 Youard Lecture on Welsh Legal and Social History

University of Swansea

2 December 2011

I HAD the privilege of delivering the David Lloyd George Memorial Lecture in Criccieth on 22 June 2006 on "The Contribution of Welsh Lawyers" and published in the *Transactions of the Honourable Society of Cymmrodorion*, 2006.[1]

I hope tonight I will be able to deal with a further contribution, perhaps with more modest subjects, given that from chambers in this city, two Attorney Generals commenced their professional careers.

In another Cymmrodorion Lecture in Cardiff in 1982, Lord Edmund-Davies, one of my mentors, singled out two Welsh judges as of outstanding quality – David Jenkins of Hensol (1582-1663) and the other, Lord Atkin of Aberdovey who he believed to be a flawless judge. Need I say more?

Jenkins is less well known, but as a parliamentarian for over 50 years, I report that when Jenkins was brought from the Tower of London to the House of Commons to be examined, he refused to kneel calling the place "a den of thieves". When the House voted him guilty of treason, he made the immortal reply: "So be it. I shall go to my death with the Bible under one arm and Magna Carta under the other".

[1] Lord Morris of Aberavon, KG, QC, 'The Contribution of Welsh Lawyers': The David Lloyd George Memorial Lecture 2006, (2007) 13 *Transactions of the Honourable Society of the Cymmrodorion* [NS], 213–224.

Both of Edmund-Davies's favourite judges manifested their integrity and independence.

My experience as a common law barrister, specialising in criminal law, provided little training for the breadth and frequency of the advice Her Majesty's Government expected of me as a law officer in matters of international law. Although I mentioned it when I appeared before the International Court of Justice at the Hague as Attorney General, I discounted the long-forgotten but enjoyable experience many years earlier as a student when I attended a summer course at the Academy of International Law, next door.

The problems of armed intervention by the UK in Kosovo dominated a good part of my life in 1998 and 1999.

It is a convention that not only is the advice of the Law Officers not made public, but also that their advice has even been sought is not revealed.

I have negotiated at considerable length with the Cabinet Secretary what I could disclose in my book *Fifty Years in Politics and the Law*[2] and in response to representations I have limited considerably what I would otherwise have written. Whatever the position in the past, the Cabinet Secretary gave permission for one of my successors, Lord Goldsmith, to disclose at the Chilcott Inquiry his advice, without prejudice, "given the exceptional nature of the Iraq Inquiry".

One of the unintended consequences of this decision was that repeatedly in the evidence given by Lord Goldsmith, my role in Kosovo was referred to, my apparent role in the drafting of earlier UN Resolutions and the precedents I either created or acted upon.

Edwards, on "The Attorney General, Politics and the Public Interest" rejected an absolute prohibition on disclosure and says, "Readiness to disclose... must enhance those independent qualities of their office."

Nevertheless, in my book I have reduced the account of my role to a narrative form so as to take into account official views.

What were the UK's and other NATO countries' problems in Kosovo?

It could be said, with some force, that there was no direct UN authority for armed intervention in that part of Yugoslavia.

---

[2] Lord Morris of Aberavon, *Fifty Years in Politics and the Law* (Cardiff, 2011).

Article 2(4) of the UN Charter prohibits "The threat or use of force against the territorial integrity or political independence of any state." That prohibition was reinforced in the context of Kosovo by the legal duty of NATO (and all other) states not to interfere in the civic strife in another state.

As an exception to the general prohibition on the use of force, the United Nations Charter permits the use of force in two circumstances: first, in self-defence; and second with the authorisation of the Security Council. Neither provided a justification for the NATO bombing campaign which took place over a period of ten weeks.

The right of self-defence is set out in Article 51 of the UN Charter. While it could be argued that there can be a degree of elasticity in what is self-defence, such as anticipating an attack, there was no element of this in Kosovo.

The second exception to the use of force in the UN Charter is the authorisation of the Security Council.

Neither Resolution 1199, adopted on 23 September 1998, nor Resolution 1203, adopted on 24 October 1998, authorised military action by NATO in the subsequent "Operation Allied Force". It has been strongly argued that "Operation Allied Force" cannot be justified on the basis of Security Council authorisation.

The Foreign and Commonwealth Office rightly told the House of Commons Select Committee that it had been clear since June 1998 that China and Russia would veto in the Security Council any authorisation for Chapter VII Intervention.

Eminent professors have argued that the analysis of the text of the UN Charter yields no clear justification for the NATO action; on the contrary, they argued that the action was unlawful.

Professor Adam Roberts told the Foreign Affairs Committee of the House of Commons (4th Report: Kosovo: June 2000) that "in strict terms of black letter international law" NATO's actions "were not demonstrably and beyond reasonable doubt legal, but equally were not illegal". The late Professor Sir Iain Brownlie, QC, who had appeared for Yugoslavia at the Hague Court on an action on this issue on 11 May 1999 and Professor (now Judge at the court) Sir Christopher Greenwood, QC and who was my second counsel in the case, took opposite views on the legality of the NATO actions.

Security Council Resolutions, although falling short of authorisation, could be argued as supportive of the NATO allies' position.

UN Security Council Resolution 1199, already referred to, called for a cease-fire, recognising "the impending humanitarian catastrophe" and affirmed there was a threat to peace and security.

UN Security Council Resolution 1203 could be said to be tacitly supporting the use of force.

A draft Resolution, proposed by Russia on 26 March 1999 which would have condemned NATO military action was rejected by 12 votes to 3. Russian failure could be interpreted as approval of that action.

UN Security Council Resolution 1244 of 10 June 1999 authorised the international security presence in Kosovo to exercise "all necessary means" to fulfil its responsibilities. This could be taken to imply *post facto* approval of military action.

Professor Chinkin argued before the House of Commons Foreign Affairs Committee:

> Arguments for the legality of NATO's actions in Yugoslavia are strengthened by taking all these actions together: the Security Council recognised the situation in Kosovo as warranting Chapter VII action; it imposed such measures as it could get agreement on; prior to the bombing it affirmed the ongoing actions of various European organisations, the EU, the OSCE and NATO, that did not involve the use of force, when it could take no stronger measures itself it did not condemn the regional agency that did so act; and subsequently to the action it endorsed the political agreement.

But she remained dubious these were sufficient grounds to regard NATO's actions as lawful.

I understand her argument.

While I welcomed the initiatives that I have set out, I would wish to make it clear that I was not relying on Security Council authorisation, although I regarded the actions taken by the Security Council, so far as they went, as helpful.

The Secretary of State for Defence, George Robertson, MP, told the House of Commons on 25 March 1999:

> We are in no doubt that NATO is acting within international law. Our legal justification rests upon the accepted principle that force may be used

> in extreme circumstances to avert a humanitarian catastrophe. These circumstances clearly exist in Kosovo.
>
> The use of force in such circumstances can be justified as an exceptional measure in support of purposes laid down by the Security Council, but without the Security Council's express authorisation, when that is the only means to avert an immediate and overwhelming catastrophe. UN Security Council Resolution 1199 clearly calls on the Yugoslavian authorities to take immediate steps to cease their repression of the Kosovo Albanians and to enter into a meaningful dialogue, leading to a negotiated political solution.[3]

I believe this was the position adopted by the other NATO nations. The right to intervene is not unlimited. It relies on two elements. Prior prescription of policies or "purposes" by the Security Council and the existence of an imminent humanitarian catastrophe that can, and can only, be averted by the use of force. It is not an assertion of a simple right of humanitarian intervention.

There had to be three elements in the Secretary of State's formulating of principle:

1. prior determination by the Security Council of a grave crisis, threatening international peace and security;
2. articulation by the Security Council of specific policies for the resolution of the crisis, the implementation of which can be secured or furthered by armed intervention;
3. an imminent humanitarian catastrophe which it is believed can be averted by the use of force and *only* by the use of force.

In addition, intervention had to be by a multi-national force.

When I had to consider the matter in 1998, as a common lawyer I looked for precedents for any action we took. However, another Law Officer from this area, Sir Samuel Evans, later President of the Probate, Divorce and Admiralty Division of the High Court, once said:

> Precedents handed down from earlier days should be treated as guides to lead and not as shackles to bind.

---

[3] Hansard HC 25 March 1999: Cols. 616–617.

My predecessors in 1991 had concluded on the particular facts before them that there was a respectable argument to justify the use of force on the grounds of an overwhelming necessity to avoid a humanitarian disaster in Iraq One.

They authorised "no fly zones" applied to Saddam Hussein's aircraft to prevent him from murdering the Kurdish population in the north of Iraq and the Marsh Arabs in the south.

The principles we adopted in Kosovo were the same as those relied upon earlier in Iraq by my predecessors. However, our earlier actions in Iraq One could be described as "passive". In Kosovo we were going further, as our proposals were undoubtedly pro-active. It is one thing to use force to guard the airspace. We were going much further in authorising air bombing night after night. However, these "purposes" were the same.

International law is not static. It develops through the agreement of new treaties and other international instruments, and through the evolution of customary law. Moreover, it is at least arguable that the preponderant will of the international community ought not to be held to ransom by the exercise of the veto or threat of the exercise of the veto by a minority, or indeed only one of the permanent Members of the Security Council.

Professor Greenwood put it very succinctly to the Foreign Affairs Committee referred to earlier:

> an interpretation of international law which would forbid intervention to prevent something as terrible as the Holocaust, unless a permanent Member could be persuaded to lift its veto, would be contrary to the principles on which modern international law is based as well as flying in the face of developments of the last fifty years.

Professor Lowe told the Committee that NATO action (if a break of a fifty year old Charter) was "consonant with the way international law was developing."

Professor Greenwood argued that the very short time scale over which the new practice had been apparent was unsurprising in international law, where a custom could develop much more quickly than in domestic law. Moreover he argued that customary law formed a much more important part of international law.

Having heard arguments to the contrary, the Select Committee concluded that

> at the very least, the doctrine of humanitarian intervention has a tenuous basis in current international customary law and this renders NATO action legally questionable.

They further concluded that, faced with the threat of a veto in the Security Council by Russia and China, the NATO allies

> did all they could to make the military intervention in Kosovo as compliant with the tenets of international law as possible.

Professor Chinkin put it:

> The actions have a legitimacy, if not strict legality, under international law.

Justice Holmes's dictum to the U.S. Supreme Court was quoted:

> A constitution is not a suicide pact.

The Select Committee reached a conclusion

> that NATO's military action, if of dubious legality in the current state of international law, was justified on moral grounds.

I think I have said enough, without setting out further the arguments, to explain a little of the legal and moral quagmire in which I was operating.

How did I approach the problem?

I had to give the legal advice. The military, who had to act in pursuit of the decisions of their political masters, had the biggest interest of all in ensuring the legality of their actions. They needed that protection.

My approach, like many other conclusions when adapting law to the facts, was rather a simplistic one. If a burglar, having entered your house, was intent on setting it on fire, and the local constable seemed reluctant to act, you could not just wait and complain to the chief constable, let alone to the police committee – you had to act. Some of the lessons of the Holocaust, which haunts so many of us, should have been learnt. International inactivity has unacceptable memories.

Sometimes the best one could do was to say I believed we had 'a respectable argument' or 'an arguable case'. This is Foreign Office speak and indeed, law officers' speak. It implies that we cannot be one hundred per cent sure. Even in common law, we frequently cannot be one hundred per cent sure, but we do have fairly firm indicators to help us to steer our case to safety. There is an element of constructiveness about interpreting international law. Things are more fluid than in domestic law, and new situations demand the means to deal with them, which had not been contemplated by the founding fathers.

I was reacting to an international nightmare where thousands of lives were being lost; Kosovars were being killed and maimed by the Serbs. It became NATO's task to prevent more of these human tragedies and restore refugees to their homes.

I was very mindful of the words of Security Council Resolution 1199 (1998) which explicitly recognised the existence of a humanitarian catastrophe and went on

> should concrete measures be taken.... The Security Council would consider further actions and additional measures to maintain or restore peace and stability in the area.

I emphasised that it was important such consideration took place before military action was taken.

I was clear in my own mind that we must be able to show we had respected the pre-eminent rules of the Security Council in international peace and security and give it every chance to deal with the deteriorating situation.

Unfortunately no such action was forthcoming until United Nations Security Council Resolution 1244 of 10 June 1999, which as I have related was *post facto*.

In the meantime, in April 1999 the UN Commission on Human Rights had carried a resolution condemning Yugoslavian actions in Kosovo by a majority of 44:1 and 6 abstentions.

I believed there was a respectable argument for action in Kosovo. I had been satisfied that the three criteria I considered necessary were met:

- There had to be convincing evidence, generally accepted by the international community as a whole, of extreme humanitarian distress on a large scale, requiring immediate action and urgent relief.

- There was, in all the circumstances, no practical alternative to the use of force, if lives were to be saved.

- The proposed use of force was necessary and proportionate to the aim being pursued (the relief of humanitarian need) and was strictly limited in time and scope to this aim, i.e., it was the minimum necessary to achieve this aim.

In the absence of a Security Council Resolution giving explicit authority for action, our actions would be weighed against these criteria.

There was no convincing evidence, indeed no evidence at all, of Milosevic's compliance with the Security Council resolution. In fact his continuing conduct was a 'material breach' of Resolution 1199 (1998) and no doubt also exacerbated the humanitarian problems. But the fact of material breach did not of itself authorise the use of force in this case: in this case the legal argument was that the use of force was justified to prevent a humanitarian catastrophe. The material breach argument (i.e., material breach of UNSCRs establishing a ceasefire) was of course the legal argument relied on to justify the use of force against Iraq in 1998 and 2003 (and earlier). There was agreement among colleagues on the use of force, provided it was deemed necessary, that it was proportionate, and strictly limited to this objective.

My colleagues accepted from the beginning that particular targets for any bombing that took place would have to be assessed against these criteria.

At all times the need for proportionality was clear, i.e., that the proposed use of force was the minimum necessary to achieve that objective. Anything beyond this would not have any legal basis.

The role of government lawyers, and myself in particular, was to approve the legality of air strikes from the UK.

There would be no basis for some general or ulterior motive, such as reprisal or punishment, nor could it be designed to degrade Yugoslavian military capability. Regime change would likewise have no legal basis.

On a daily basis, wherever I was during the whole of this period, officials of the Ministry of Defence would come to me with their proposed attacks. Sunday night at my home was a favourite time. My presence at mayor-making in Port Talbot was interrupted by an unplanned visit, via St. Athan's Airfield, to seek my advice.

I examined all the proposals in considerable detail. I was fortunate in the advice I received from my own staff. As the campaign went on, the proposers came to understand my approach and what I was likely to query. In the event there was normally an agreement, but I did query and warn on some difficult targets.

Casualties had to be assessed as low. There had to be a definite military advantage (Article 57 of the Additional Protocol of the Geneva Convention); and where there was a choice of military targets, the object to be selected should cause the least damage to civilians and to civilian objects. A significant problem for me to advise on was where there was a duel use of infrastructure by both military and civilians, e.g., a railway line or train.

My concerns were not theoretical or academic. I believed we could expect close scrutiny after the event. This scrutiny need not stop in Parliament. The UK courts had jurisdiction under the Geneva Conventions. Prosecutions could be brought against anyone, whether in the UK or not, who committed or aided, abetted or procured the commission by any other person of grave breaches of the Conventions. The International Criminal Tribunal for the former Yugoslavia had power to prosecute persons 'violating the laws and customs of war'. Unjustified attacks on civilian property and unjustified casualties to civilians were very much within the scope of that court. We could expect any NATO actions which came close to the edge of lawfulness to be brought to the attention of the (independent) prosecutor. Our actions would come within the ambit of the International Court of Justice, the European Court of Justice, or the European Court of Human Rights. Litigation in any of these would quickly bring under judicial scrutiny the legal justification for our actions against Yugoslavia. The outcome of that scrutiny could not be guaranteed.

All this reinforced my belief in the continued need for the most scrupulous adherence to legal requirements. As the campaign intensified, we had to be careful that we kept in the forefront of our minds the legal constraints which govern the use of force by our servicemen and women and those who authorised them. I believed that the limits of the legal basis for our actions in Yugoslavia and the constraints which apply to the use of force should be constantly and carefully kept in view as the campaign developed.

I have always believed, and I have given evidence to this effect to Select Committees, that the role of the Attorney General is to be candid with his or her employers – and they must be able, if they wish, to rely on his advice. The Attorney General is not there to please, but to give sound advice.

I surmised that it was irritating to the Prime Minister and his immediate advisers that his chief lawyer was forever crying wolf, and operating a most conservative interpretation of the law.

At the end of the campaign, as I have recalled in my book, when I was due to go on leave after about 68 days conflict, I had received a further application involving a considerable escalation of the military aims, which I will not detail. Suffice to say I did not give my blessing to that particular proposal. I went away to Scotland to fish, and I was not a party to the permission given the following day.

No one was more relieved than I was to hear on TV in Scotland that Milosevic had caved in and that the war was over. The American refusal to involve ground troops other than in a permissive environment probably encouraged Milosevic to hold out longer against NATO. It was only when the momentum started to build up that he backed down.

On 9 March 1999, Baroness Symons, an FCO Minister, replied in Parliament:

> My Lords, all NATO operations must have a basis in international law. Each case needs to be looked at on its own merits. In many cases a United Nations Security Council resolution would be needed to authorise the use of force. But force may be used to defend a non-NATO state... or, in exceptional circumstances, to avert an immediate and overwhelming humanitarian catastrophe.
>
> My Lords, cases have arisen, for example, in northern Iraq in 1991, when, in the light of all the circumstances, a limited use of force has been justifiable as the only means to avert an overwhelming humanitarian catastrophe in support of purposes laid down by the Security Council but without the Council's express authorisation. Such cases, by their very nature must be exceptional and would depend on an objective assessment of the factual circumstances at the time and of the relevant decisions of the Security Council bearing on the situation. It is important to stress that all NATO decisions are taken by consensus. Not a single member of the alliance can force the other members to act if the allies are opposed. All

> our allies would not agree a NATO operation, I believe, unless they considered it was in accordance with international law.

My warnings about the possibility of the UK being hauled before a court bore fruit and I was summoned back from an international legal conference in Trinidad to lead for our defence in an application brought by Yugoslavia against the UK and nine other NATO countries for the equivalent of an injunction to stop the bombing, i.e., an indication of provisional measures.

The first pillar of our defence was one of jurisdiction – I suggested that the application by Yugoslavia was an abuse of the process of the court, as the present Federal Republic of Yugoslavia was not a party to the statute of the court, and had not filed to apply for membership of the United Nations when it succeeded the former Yugoslavia. Only a party to the statute could make a valid declaration under the appropriate provisions of the statute: as the FRY had only deposited an acceptance of the court's compulsory jurisdiction only three days before the present application, and so under the rules it could not provide even a prima facie basis for the exercise of the jurisdiction of the court. There were other jurisdictional objections too.

I continued my argument based on the overwhelming humanitarian disaster that had been witnessed in Kosovo. I quoted Mrs Ogata, the United Nations High Commissioner for Refugees, when she briefed in person the members of the Security Council on 5 May, a week after these proceedings were started:

> The situation of women, men and children fleeing the Province of Kosovo and Metohija, in the Federal Republic of Yugoslavia, is increasingly desperate. Kosovo is being emptied – brutally and methodically – of its ethnic Albanian population. In the last three days alone about 37,000 new refugees and internally displaced people have arrived in Albania, the former Yugoslav Republic of Macedonia, and the Republic of Montenegro. More trains with thousands of refugees have arrived last night at the Yugoslav/Macedonian border. Ethnic cleansing and mass forced expulsions are yielding their tragic results faster than we can respond . . . fragile and unprepared countries are bearing the brunt of one of the largest refugee flows Europe has seen in the twentieth century. Seven hundred thousand people have already been forced to leave their homes.
>
> This refugee crisis is not new. Last year, more than a quarter of all asylum requests in Europe were by people from Kosovo. Up to 23 March,

> when UNHCR had to reluctantly leave the province following a decision of the United Nations Security Coordinator, it was providing assistance to 400,000 people displaced or otherwise affected by fighting inside the province, and to 90,000 refugees and displaced people outside Kosovo.

I adopted the words of the UK's permanent representative when he addressed the Security Council on 24 March, describing our military action as:

> an exceptional measure to prevent an overwhelming humanitarian catastrophe . . . under present circumstances in Kosovo there is convincing evidence that such a catastrophe is imminent. Renewed acts of repression by the authorities of the Federal Republic of Yugoslavia would cause further loss of civilian life and would lead to displacement of the civilian population on a large scale and in hostile conditions. Every means short of force has been tried to avert this situation . . . The force now proposed is directed exclusively to averting a humanitarian catastrophe, and is the minimum judged necessary for that purpose.

I ended my speech by formally requesting the court to summarily dismiss the request for the indication of provisional measures submitted by the Federal Republic of Yugoslavia.

The judgment of the court in respect of the case of the applicant and the nine defendant countries was delivered on 2 June 1999 in the following terms:

> In an order issued in the case concerning legality in the use of force (*Federal Republic of Yugoslavia (FRY)* v *the United Kingdom*) the court rejected by twelve votes to three the request for an indication of provisional measures submitted by the Federal Republic of Yugoslavia.

As we had learned, Yugoslavia had not deposited its declaration of the acceptance of the compulsory jurisdiction of the court within the obligatory twelve months prior to the filing of its application. It had only done so three days before it brought its dispute to the court.

The court concluded that in the circumstances it had no jurisdiction on the case, and that it lacked prima facie jurisdiction to entertain Yugoslavia's application and 'it cannot therefore indicate any provisional measures whatsoever'.

The court could not adjudicate on the main issue – the legality of our actions. Much as I was relieved by our success on the jurisdictional point, I was disappointed that the opportunity could not be taken to judge legality of actions such as ours and other NATO countries.

Regrettably the Foreign Affairs Committee in Paragraph 136 of the Report referred to is erroneous in its comment that the UK "Did not contest the substantive issue". Having consulted my team, we are confident that in addition to the jurisdictional point, our pleadings and oral arguments encompassed a much wider submission and we did not withdraw any submissions regarding the legality of our actions.

Before Kosovo and Iraq One, litigation about the use of force was in practice highly unlikely. I believe my predecessors who were law officers had mentioned the possibility, but more as a remote threat than a realistic prospect.

I believed my warnings were justified to the hilt. The whole episode proves the value of the independent judgment of a law officer.

Looking back on the events in Kosovo, it is regrettable that so far there has been no systematic attempt to further develop the theory and practice of humanitarian intervention – the basic criterion for intervention is that the violations of human rights within a particular state have reached a situation where they shock the conscience of humanity. Action was taken in Kosovo by a number of states who justified their use of force with no explicit Security Council authority.

The late Lord Bingham, in his authoritative book *The Rule of Law* while analysing in some detail his criticisms of the basis for action in Iraq II, merely states as regards the basis of our action in Kosovo:

> There is controversy whether force may be exceptionally used to avert an overwhelming humanitarian catastrophe but otherwise the law under the charter is clear: save in self-defence, force may be used if authorised by the Security Council but not otherwise.[4]

Professor Christine Gray, in her book *International Law and the Use of Force*[5] relates to some disagreements on the interpretation of Article 2 [4]

---

[4] Tom Bingham, *The Rule of Law*, (London, 2010), p. 121.

[5] Christine Gray, *International Law and the Use of Force* (3rd Ed., Oxford, 2008).

of the UN Charter and whether new circumstances have caused it to be evolved since 1945.

The Secretary General of the UN in his 1999 Report has warned against the enforcement action without Security Council authorisation "as it had the prime responsibility".[6] On another occasion he had said:

> Emerging slowly but I believe surely, is an international norm against the violent repression of minorities that will and must take precedence over concerns of state sovereignty.[7]

Professor Gray concludes:

> Thus the controversy over the legality of humanitarian intervention continues.

The House of Commons Foreign Affairs Select Committee concludes:

> We support the FCO in its aim of establishing in the United Nations new principles governing humanitarian intervention.

It appears from Baroness Northover's reply in the House of Lords (7 November 2011) that there does not seem to be much progress.

I conclude in my book:

> It will continue to be a matter of controversy, whether a new doctrine of intervention without Security Council authority has been established. The validity of the doctrine will be strengthened by similar action and I foresee it becoming established as customary international law. The greater the number of states to validate the doctrine, the greater its claim to be customary international law.[8]

[6] Ibid., p. 48

[7] Ibid., p. 46.

[8] Lord Morris of Aberavon, *Fifty Years in Politics and the Law*, p. 220.

DADLEUON DICHELLGAR A DATGANOLI

Hanes yr Ymgyrch dros Awdurdodaeth Gymreig

Thomas Glyn Watkin

GADEWCH imi ddechrau drwy ddiolch i'r Sefydliad Materion Cymreig am ei wahoddiad caredig i draddodi ei ddarlith flynyddol yma yn yr Eisteddfod eleni. Mae'n anrhydedd i mi yn bersonol, a hefyd yn gyfle i gyfranogi o ddadl sy'n bwysig ar hyn o bryd ym mywyd y genedl.

Flwyddyn yn ôl, cefais y fraint o gyfranogi o sgwrs ar faes yr Eisteddfod ynglŷn ag awdurdodaeth i Gymru, sgwrs a oedd wedi ei threfnu gan Gymdeithas y Cyfreithwyr. Yn y cyfamser mae Pwyllgor Materion Cyfansoddiadol a Deddfwriaethol y Cynulliad Cenedlaethol wedi cynnal ymchwiliad i'r cwestiwn,[1] ac y mae Llywodraeth Cymru hithau wedi lansio ymgynghoriad ar yr union bwnc.[2] Braf oedd gweld y nifer helaeth o ymatebion a gafodd eu derbyn gan y Pwyllgor Materion Cyfansoddiadol a gweld bod cymaint o ddiddordeb bellach ym mhynciau cyfansoddiadol ymhlith y Cymry. Bydd yn ddiddorol gweld beth fydd canlyniadau'r holl waith sydd ar y gweill ar hyn o bryd.

Nid hwn, fodd bynnag, yw'r tro cyntaf i gyfundrefn farnwrol ar wahân i Gymru gael ei thrafod, ac y mae'r cysyniad o awdurdodaeth wedi bod yn bwysig mewn nifer o ddadleuon ynglŷn â sefyllfa gyfreithiol Cymru fwy nag unwaith. Yn sgil y Rhyfel Byd Cyntaf, a map gwleidyddol Ewrop yn cael ei ail-lunio, a hyd yn oed map gwleidyddol Ynysoedd Prydain yn cael ei ailstrwythuro wrth i Weriniaeth Iwerddon ymadael â'r Deyrnas Unedig, fe gododd y cwestiwn hwn: a ddylai pob rhan o'r hyn oedd ar ôl o'r Deyrnas Unedig gael ei chyfundrefn farnwrol ei hun, hynny yw, gwahanol awdurdodaethau i Ogledd Iwerddon, yr Alban, ac i Gymru a Lloegr fel gwledydd ar wahân? Yn ystod trafodaethau Cynhadledd y Llefarydd, sefydlwyd is-bwyllgor o dan yr Arglwydd Stuart o Wortley i ystyried y

---

[1] Gweler *Cynulliad Cenedlaethol Cymru: Y Pwyllgor Materion Cyfansoddiadol a Deddfwriaethol: Ymchwiliad i sefydlu awdurdodaeth ar wahân i Gymru* – Rhagfyr 2011; *Ymatebion i'r ymgynghoriad* – Mawrth 2012.

[2] Gweler *Llywodraeth Cymru: Dogfen Ymgynghori: Awdurdodaeth Gyfreithiol ar Wahân ar gyfer Cymru* – Rhif WG-15109 (27 Mawrth 2012).

pwnc arbennig hwn. Yn y pen draw, ni chafwyd ateb bendant i'r cwestiwn, ond ymhlith yr argymhellion a ystyriwyd, awgrymodd yr is-bwyllgor fod cwestiwn cyfundrefn farnwrol ar wahân i Gymru yn un a ddylai gael ei ateb gan ddeddfwrfa Gymreig, pryd bynnag y byddai un yn bodoli.[3] O safbwynt 1920, mae hyn yn edrych yn debyg iawn i gic eithriadol am yr ystlys, ond yn awr, wrth gwrs, mae'r bêl yn ôl ar y cae, ac mae'n ddiddorol cofio bod yr adroddiad yn 20au'r ganrif ddiwethaf wedi mynd ymlaen i ddweud y dylai unrhyw statud datganoli yn y dyfodol gynnwys cymal yn datgan yn glir y dylai Senedd San Steffan ddeddfu i roi cyfundrefn farnwrol i Gymru pryd bynnag y gofynnai deddfwrfa Gymreig amdani.[4]

Ar y pryd, yr oedd tipyn o gefnogaeth ymhlith cyfreithwyr y genedl i'r syniad o gyfundrefn farnwrol ar wahân i Gymru, yn enwedig ymhlith barnwyr a bargyfreithwyr yn y De.[5] Mae'n wir hefyd fod rhai o swyddogion y llywodraeth Brydeinig yn Llundain wedi dadlau'n gryf i'r gwrthwyneb, gan gynnwys Syr Claud Schuster, Ysgrifennydd Parhaol Swyddfa'r Arglwydd Ganghellor.[6] Yr oedd Schuster wedi cael ei benodi i'w swydd yn ifanc iawn, yn ei ddeugeiniau, ac fe arhosodd yn y swydd am dros chwarter canrif. O ganlyniad, cafodd gryn ddylanwad fel gwas sifil, ac fwy nag unwaith defnyddiodd ei ddylanwad i wrthwynebu datblygiadau cyfreithiol i Gymru. Ei ddadl ym 1920 oedd nad oedd yn bosibl i Gymru gael cyfundrefn farnwrol ar wahân i Loegr oherwydd nad oedd gan Gymru ei chyfreithiau ei hun. Nid oedd corff o gyfraith Gymreig yn bodoli yn yr

[3] "the only competent judge of the strength and purpose of the Welsh desires for separate judicial arrangements from those of England would, in our opinion, be a Welsh legislature or other legislative authority specially constituted under a scheme of Devolution to represent the people of Wales". National Archives, LCO 2/507, Draft Report, ¶ 11.

[4] "we think that the creation of a Welsh judiciary should be effected if and when the Welsh legislature shall ask for it. It, if so desired, should be a Judiciary equal in independence to that of Scotland, with no appeal save to the House of Lords or its successor as the Supreme Appellate tribunal of the United Kingdom"; National Archives, LCO 2/507, Draft Report, ¶ 22.

[5] Llythyr (24/2/20) oddi wrth Syr Claud Schuster at Ei Anrhydedd y Barnwr Rowland Rowlands, "I believe the scheme [ar gyfer cyfundrefn farnwrol ar wahân dros Gymru] has a powerful backing": National Archives, LCO 2/507.

[6] Gweler, Syr John Thomas, "Legal Wales: Its Modern Origins and its Role after Devolution – National Identity, the Welsh Language and Parochialism" yn T.G. Watkin (gol.), *Legal Wales: Its Past, Its Future* (Caerdydd, 2001), 113–166.

un modd ag yr oedd corff gwahanol o gyfraith yn bodoli yn yr Alban a Gogledd Iwerddon. Defnyddiodd yr un ddadl tua chwarter canrif yn ddiweddarach wrth drafod gyda'i gyd-weision sifil gwestiwn Ysgrifennydd Gwladol i Gymru,[7] a gellir gweld i ryw raddau ddylanwad Schuster ar yr adroddiad ym 1920 wrth ystyried y cysylltiad yn yr argymhellion rhwng yr achos dros gyfundrefn farnwrol a bodolaeth deddfwrfa Gymreig, hynny yw sefydliad gyda phwerau i greu corff o gyfreithiau Cymreig.

Y mae'r ddadl yn un ddiddorol, oherwydd y mae'n gwneud cysylltiad clir rhwng y syniad o awdurdodaeth a chorff o gyfraith, ond hefyd y mae'r ddadl yn rhyfedd wrth ystyried hanes cyfreithiol Cymru yn y genhedlaeth gynt. Oherwydd yr oedd yna reswm am gefnogaeth barnwyr a bargyfreithwyr y De i'r syniad o gyfundrefn farnwrol ar wahân, rheswm yn deillio o'r hyn a ddigwyddodd ddeugain mlynedd yn gynharach wrth i Senedd San Steffan ddeddfu i Gymru ar wahân i Loegr am y tro cyntaf. Y ddeddf oedd y Ddeddf Cau ar y Sul (Cymru), [Sunday Closing (Wales) Act] 1881.

Wrth i'r ddeddfwriaeth arfaethedig gael ei thrafod yn Nhŷ'r Cyffredin ym 1880 a 1881, ymhlith ei gwrthwynebwyr yr oedd yr Aelod Seneddol Ceidwadol dros Bridport, Edward Warton. O ran egwyddor, ei ddadl oedd nad oedd yn bosibl deddfu i Gymru ar wahân i Loegr oherwydd yr oedd Cymru a Lloegr yn un – un diriogaeth integredig yn cael ei gwasanaethu gan un gyfundrefn farnwrol. Gan nad oedd cyfundrefn farnwrol ar wahân gan Gymru, nid oedd yn bosibl deddfu ar ei chyfer. Nid oedd Cymru yn awdurdodaeth, felly nid oedd yn bosibl iddi gael corff o gyfreithiau.[8] Ni fu'r ddadl yn llwyddiannus – fe ddaeth y Prif Weinidog ei hun, William

[7] Llythyr (18/5/44) oddi wrth Syr Claud Schuster at Syr Alan Barlow: 'the Scottish and English judicial systems are, except for the appeal to the House of Lords, wholly distinct and separate, and operate a separate jurisprudence founded on different principles with different origins. The English and Welsh system of jurisprudence is a uniform integral whole operating a system of jurisprudence which is uniform, and has regard to the same principles, and springs from the same origins. The substantive law of England and Wales is not similar but the same, except for some minor immaterial differences.' National Archives, LCO 2/3214.

[8] Parl. Deb. (Cyfres 3) cyf. 253 (1880) HC 30 Mehefin: "were they to have fractional or national legislation? They all highly respected and loved Wales, but, after all, it was but a small part of England" (Edward Warton). "But he did not know that it had been hitherto recognized that Wales should be treated in a different way from other portions of the Kingdom" (Arthur Peel).

Gladstone, i'r Tŷ i gefnogi'r Bil,[9] ond mae'n amlwg bod y ddadl wedi cael effaith ar yr aelodau o Gymru ac ar gyfreithwyr Cymru wrth iddynt hwy ystyried a chofio bod Cymru wedi meddu ar ei llysoedd barn ei hun hyd at 1830 – Llysoedd y Sesiwn Fawr – ac os oedd angen cyfundrefn farnwrol ar wahân ar Gymru er mwyn ennill ei deddfau ei hun, efallai bryd hynny yr oedd yn amser i'w hailennill.[10]

Felly, yn 80au'r bedwaredd ganrif ar bymtheg, y ddadl oedd nad oedd yn bosibl i Gymru feddu ar ei chyfreithiau ei hun gan nad oedd ganddi hi ei llysoedd barn ei hun, a ddeugain mlynedd yn ddiweddarach yr ateb i'r deisyfiad am lysoedd barn Cymreig oedd nad oedd hynny'n bosibl oherwydd nad oedd gan Gymru ei chyfreithiau ei hun. Naill ai mae elfen gylchog yn y ddadl, neu – ac yn bwysig iawn o ran y sefyllfa sydd ohoni – nid yw'n bosibl cael y naill heb y llall, hynny yw – eto gan adlewyrchu argymhellion adroddiad 1920 – mae corff o gyfreithiau ar wahân yn galw am gyfundrefn farnwrol ar wahân.

Yr wyf wedi osgoi hyd yn hyn lawer o ddefnydd o'r gair *awdurdodaeth* – a hynny am reswm. Mae yna fwy nag un ystyr i'r gair, ac y mae hynny wedi caniatáu i'r gair gael ei ddefnyddio mewn modd ystwyth weithiau sydd yn cuddio natur gylchog rhai o'r dadleuon yn erbyn datblygiadau cyfreithiol ar gyfer Cymru. Gall *awdurdodaeth* olygu 'tiriogaeth a chanddi ei chyfreithiau ei hun'; hefyd gall olygu 'tiriogaeth a chanddi ei chyfundrefn farnwrol ei hun'. O ganlyniad, gellir dweud – fel yn y 1880au – na all Cymru gael ei deddfwriaeth ei hun oherwydd nad yw Cymru'n awdurdodaeth, a hefyd, fel ym 1920, na all Cymru gael ei chyfundrefn farnwrol ei hun oherwydd nad yw Cymru'n awdurdodaeth. Mae'r ffaith bod y gair yn gallu cael ei ddefnyddio mewn mwy nag un ystyr yn caniatáu iddo gael ei ddefnyddio mewn modd sydd yn arwynebol gyson, ond mewn gwirionedd y mae'r cysondeb nid yn unig yn arwynebol ond yn ffug – ac y mae hynny wedi caniatáu iddo gael ei ddefnyddio mewn modd eithaf dichellgar o bryd i'w gilydd er mwyn cyfiawnhau gwrthod i Gymru ddatblygiadau cyfreithiol a ganiatawyd, er enghraifft, i'r Alban.

Ac yn anffodus, yn y degawdau a ddilynodd, cafodd yr Alban ei defnyddio fel llinyn mesur bron bob tro y cafodd cwestiwn ei godi ynglŷn â darpariaeth gyfreithiol wahanol i Gymru. Ar ddiwedd y 30au, ychydig cyn

[9] Parl. Deb. (Cyfres 3) cyf. 260 (1881) HC 4 Mai: colofnau 1772–1775.

[10] "Wales should have restored to it the separate judiciary it once had": *Western Mail*, Dydd Gwener, 26 Mawrth 1920.

yr Ail Ryfel Byd, gwrthododd y Llywodraeth ganiatáu i Gymru gael Ysgrifennydd Gwladol yn yr un modd ag yr oedd gan yr Alban. Yn sgil cynnydd sylweddol yn y ddarpariaeth arbennig ar gyfer yr Alban, ateb y Prif Weinidog, Neville Chamberlain, oedd bod cymharu Cymru â'r Alban yn amherthnasol, oherwydd bod gan yr Alban gyfundrefnau cyfreithiol a gweinyddol hyd yn oed cyn i Swyddfa'r Alban gael ei chreu. Yr oedd Cymru ar y llaw arall wedi cael ei hymgorffori â Lloegr yn yr unfed ganrif ar bymtheg heb unrhyw gyfraith na chyfundrefn weinyddol a oedd yn haeddu sylw gweinidog arbennig.[11] Mae'n amlwg bod cymharu Cymru â'r Alban yn arwain at gymhariaeth anffafriol ar y sail bod yr Alban eisoes yn awdurdodaeth ar wahân.

Ar ddiwedd yr Ail Ryfel Byd, gofynnodd holl Aelodau Seneddol Cymru, gyda chymeradwyaeth rhai aelodau Cymreig yn Nhŷ'r Arglwyddi, am i'r cwestiwn o Ysgrifennydd Gwladol i Gymru gael ei ystyried unwaith eto.[12] Plediodd y Prif Weinidog, Winston Churchill, fod y Llywodraeth yn rhy brysur gyda materion eraill i ystyried pwnc a oedd mor gymhleth – ateb eithaf teg mewn ffordd ar ddiwedd rhyfel byd.[13] Er gwaethaf hynny, yr oedd amser gan un o'r gweision sifil mwyaf ddylanwadol, Syr Alan Barlow, i ysgrifennu at Syr Claud Schuster yn Swyddfa'r Arglwydd

[11] Llythyr oddi wrth Neville Chamberlain at Morgan Jones AS (27/7/1938): "The analogy of Scotland has been advanced ... I think, however, that it must be recognised that the two cases are not parallel. For Scotland has always had different systems of law and administration from those in force in England... Wales, on the other hand, since Henry VII's (*sic*) Act of 1535, has been closely incorporated with England and there has not been, and is not now, any distinct law or administrative system calling for the attention of a separate Minister.": LlGC, *Papurau James Griffiths*, C2/1.

[12] Memorandwm oddi wrth pob un o'r 36 aelod seneddol o Gymru at y Prif Weinidog, Winston Churchill, (28/10/1943): National Archives, LCO 2/3214.

[13] Llythyr oddi wrth Winston Churchill at Megan Lloyd George AS 2/1/1945: "Thank you for your letter of November 10 regarding the proposals of the Welsh Parliamentary Party for the establishment of a Secretary of State for Wales. The matter is, as you know, receiving consideration. The difficulty is that a proposal of this nature has such far reaching implications in the administrative sphere that detailed consideration has to be given it by the many authorities concerned. These authorities are of course heavily burdened with war tasks.": LlGC, *Papurau James Griffiths*, C2/5.

Ganghellor i dynnu ei sylw at y cais.[14] Ei ofn oedd bod cyfartaledd â'r Alban yn golygu cyfundrefn farnwrol ar wahân, gan nodi bod sylwedd cyfraith yr Alban, ac nid yn unig y modd o'i gweinyddu, yn wahanol i'r hyn a oedd yn bodoli yn Lloegr, rhywbeth nad oedd yn wir am Gymru. Yn ei ateb, cyfaddefodd Schuster nad oedd llawer o bwerau gan Ysgrifennydd Gwladol yr Alban ynglŷn â gweinyddu cyfiawnder ar wahân i benodi ynadon, ond er gwaethaf hynny awgrymodd y buasai'n ddoeth cadw cwestiwn awdurdodaeth ar wahân dan sylw oherwydd yr oedd yng Nghymru hanes o'r hyn a ddisgrifiodd fel *agitation* ynglŷn â'r pwnc.[15] Efallai yr oedd yn cofio teimladau cryf cyfreithwyr y De ar ôl y Rhyfel Byd Cyntaf, ond yn eglur yr oedd yn anhapus ynglŷn â'r hyn a ddywedwyd gan Ithel Davies yn y 30au i'r perwyl y buasai angen aildrefnu cyfundrefn farnwrol Cymru yn sylfaenol pe caniateid i'r iaith Gymraeg le cyfiawn a phriodol wrth weinyddu cyfiawnder yng Nghymru,[16] geiriau a gafodd eu cyhoeddi cyn i Ddeddf Llysoedd Cymru gael ei phasio yn 1942. Mae'n eithaf amlwg y tro hwn fod y gweision sifil yn chwilio am resymau i wrthod datblygiad cyfreithiol i Gymru, ac yr oedd cymharu Cymru'r â'r Alban yn rhoi cyfle iddynt ddefnyddio'r cysyniad ystwyth o awdurdodaeth fel esgus neu reswm cyfleus i wrthod. Yr oedd perygl wrth gymharu Cymru â'r Alban, ac mae'r perygl hwnnw'n parhau, ac nid hwn yw'r unig fath o ddadl sydd yn beryglus i'w defnyddio.

Yr oedd y ddadl yn erbyn deddfu ar wahân i Gymru oherwydd nad oedd gan Gymru gyfundrefn farnwrol a'r ddadl nad oedd yn bosibl creu cyfundrefn farnwrol i Gymru oherwydd nad oedd ganddi gyfreithiau gwahanol, y ddwy ohonynt – er gwaethaf natur gylchog y rhesymeg – o

[14] Llythyr oddi wrth J.A. Barlow (Syr Alan Barlow) at Syr Claud Schuster (12/4/44): National Archives, LCO 2/3214.

[15] Memorandwm oddi wrth Syr Claud Schuster at Syr Alan Barlow (18/5/44) "It would, however, be unwise wholly to exclude from consideration the fact that there have been signs of agitation in Wales on this subject": National Archives, LCO 2/3214.

[16] Yn ei femorandwm (nodyn 15 uchod), dyfynnodd Schuster dystiolaeth Ithel Davies yn ôl Adroddiad y Comisiwn Peel (Cmd. 5065) 20/1/36, t. 371: "if the Welsh language is given its rightful and proper place in the administration of justice in Wales, there must be something like a fundamental reorganization of the judicial system in Wales to meet that measure of recognition": National Archives, LCO 2/3214.

leiaf yn ddadlau ar sail egwyddorion cyfansoddiadol. Nid ar sail egwyddor yn unig y dadleuodd y gwrthwynebwyr. O bryd i'w gilydd, cafodd y syniad o ddarpariaeth gyfreithiol Gymreig ei watwar, efallai er mwyn gwylltio'r cefnogwyr a'u hysgogi i gyfaddef mai cenedlaetholdeb oedd prif sail eu gofynion. Ym 1880 a 1881, dadleuodd Edward Warton AS yn ffyrnig yn erbyn deddfwriaeth arbennig i Gymru gan ddweud mai dim ond rhan fach o Loegr oedd Cymru, er bod rhai bobl yn tybio bod Cymru yn rhyw fath o genedl er nad oedd erioed wedi cynhyrchu mawrion o'r un fath ag Iwerddon.[17] Yn y pen draw, yr oedd y bwriad i ddeddfu i Gymru ar wahân i Loegr yn arwydd o wendid yn llygaid Edward Warton, gwendid oedd yn ildio i ddymuniadau eithafwyr – "the fads and fancies of fanatics".[18]

Mae'n amlwg bod teimladau cryf ar waith ar y ddwy ochr yn ystod dadleuon 80au'r bedwaredd ganrif ar bymtheg. Ni ellir gorbrisio gyfraniad Gladstone ac yntau'n Brif Weinidog, i lwyddiant y Bil. Yr oedd egwyddor deddfwriaeth ar wahân i Gymru yn un bwysig i'r Rhyddfrydwyr ac i Gladstone ei hun, oherwydd yn y dyfodol byddai'r Ddeddf yn sail i ddeddfwriaeth i ddatgysylltu Eglwys Loegr yng Nghymru. Ni ddigwyddodd hynny tan ychydig cyn y Rhyfel Byd Cyntaf, gyda Chymro, David Lloyd George, yn un o hoelionwyth y Llywodraeth Ryddfrydol.

Yng nghyfnod Lloyd George fel Prif Weinidog, wrth gwrs, cafodd cwestiwn awdurdodaeth ar wahân i Gymru ei ystyried fel rhan o waith Cynhadledd y Llefarydd ym 1920. Prif Weinidog clymblaid oedd Lloyd George erbyn hynny a'r Arglwydd Ganghellor yn ei lywodraeth oedd Arglwydd Birkenhead, F.E. Smith, cyn Aelod Seneddol Ceidwadol ac un o wrthwynebwyr mwyaf Lloyd George adeg ei gyllideb wir chwyldroadol ym 1909, a hefyd yn ystod yr ymgyrch i basio'r ddeddfwriaeth a ddatgysylltodd yr Eglwys yng Nghymru. Ac yntau'n Ysgrifennydd Parhaol

[17] Parl. Deb. (Cyfres 3) cyf. 253 (1880) HC., 4 Mai: "Why should they have one Sunday Closing Bill for Wales, whose population, after all, only formed a small section of the community, but who, following the example of the Irish, fancied themselves a nation, and quite as famous as Ireland, while in point of fact, the Principality was only a small part of England? Wales, certainly, had not produced great men like Ireland" (Edward Warton AS).

[18] Parl. Deb. (Cyfres 3) cyf. 253 (1880) HC., 15 Mehefin: "The great fallacy was in trying to set up different little laws all over England, breaking the United Kingdom into sections for the purpose of carrying out the fads and fancies of fanatics." (Edward Warton AS).

ar adran o'r llywodraeth, gydag F.E. Smith wrth y llyw, fe benderfynodd Syr Claud Schuster ymyrryd yng ngwaith is-bwyllgor Cynhadledd y Llefarydd a oedd yn ystyried cyfundrefn farnwrol i Gymru ym 1920. Mae'n anodd credu nad oedd y teimladau cryf a fynegodd F.E. Smith yn ystod y ddadl ar Fil yr Eglwys Gymreig ar waith unwaith eto y tu ôl i'r llenni pan ysgrifennodd Schuster at y Llefarydd, James Lowther, ym mis Chwefror 1920 i ddweud bod yr Arglwydd Ganghellor yn dymuno i Schuster roi tystiolaeth gerbron yr is-bwyllgor.[19] Rhaid cofio bod yr ohebiaeth hon yn digwydd yn yr wythnosau olaf cyn i Ddeddf yr Eglwys yng Nghymru ddod i rym ar ddiwedd mis Mawrth 1920.

Ddeng niwrnod ar ôl ysgrifennu at y Llefarydd, ysgrifennodd Schuster lythyr at un o farnwyr y Llysoedd Sirol yn y De, sef Ei Anrhydedd y Barnwr Rowland Rowlands. Yn ei lythyr, dywedodd Schuster ei fod yn deall bod yna gryn dipyn o gefnogaeth i'r syniad o gyfundrefn farnwrol wahanol i Gymru, gan gyfaddef bod y syniad i ryw raddau i'w ddymuno, ond hefyd yn cyfaddef ei bryder bod rhai o'r cynigion yn rhy eithafol, er enghraifft, Llys Apêl ar wahân.[20] Mae'n debyg mai 'pysgota' oedd Schuster yn ei lythyr i ddarganfod beth oedd cryfder y gefnogaeth am awdurdodaeth ar wahân i Gymru a beth oedd cynnwys y cynigion y byddai'r cefnogwyr yn cyflwyno i'r Is-bwyllgor. Atebodd y Barnwr Rowlands yn ddiffuant drwy roi disgrifiad trylwyr o'r hyn yr oedd nifer o'i gyd-gyfreithwyr yn dymuno ei weld.[21]

Yn syth ar ôl derbyn ateb Rowlands, mae newid agwedd yn iaith Schuster. Atebodd lythyr Rowlands ar unwaith, ateb gyda'r dyddiad 1 Mawrth 1920, gan ofyn beth oedd ar waith yn achosi'r fath ofynion, ar wahân i ryw deimlad cenedlaethol niwlog – 'vague national sentiment', a dechrau dadlau nad oedd digon o fusnes gerbron llysoedd sifil Cymru i

---

[19] Llythyr oddi wrth Syr Claud Schuster at James W. Lowther AS (13/2/20): National Archives, LCO 2/507.

[20] Llythyr (24/2/20) oddi wrth Syr Claud Schuster at Ei Anrhydedd y Barnwr Rowland Rowlands: "no doubt, within limits, the proposed change is desirable, but I have an idea that some of the proposals to be put forward – particularly those dealing with appeals etc. – are too extreme, at any rate for the present": National Archives, LCO 2/507.

[21] Llythyr oddi wrth y Barnwr R. Rowlands at Syr Claud Schuster (29/2/20): National Archives, LCO 2/507.

gyfiawnhau'r fath ddatblygiad.[22] Heb aros am ateb Rowlands, gofynnodd i B.J. Bridgeman gynnal ymchwil i gost llysoedd sirol Cymru a maint y ffioedd yr oeddent yn eu codi.[23] Mae'n debyg bod Schuster wedi cysylltu â Rowlands yn fwriadol er mwyn darganfod cryfder a natur y ddadl o blaid awdurdodaeth i Gymru er mwyn paratoi'r achos yn erbyn y fath ddatblygiad gerbron yr Is-bwyllgor. Mae'r modd yr ysgrifennodd at Rowlands ym mis Chwefror mor wahanol i'r modd a ysgrifennodd ar ddydd Gŵyl Dewi ar ôl derbyn yr wybodaeth yr oedd ei heisiau arno yn dangos mwy nag elfen o ddichell, yn enwedig wrth ystyried pa mor gyflym oedd ei ymateb pendant yn erbyn y cynllun unwaith yr oedd yr wybodaeth yn ei ddwylo. Mae'n amlwg hefyd bod Rowlands wedi deall y sefyllfa, oherwydd wrth iddo ef ymateb wythnos yn ddiweddarach, y mae'n gwadu mai teimladau cenedlaethol yn unig oedd tu ôl i'r ymgyrch am awdurdodaeth i Gymru gan restru materion ymarferol a oedd yn cefnogi datblygiad o'r fath.[24] Yn anffodus, symudodd hyn y ddadl at faterion ymarferol, yn gwmws yn ôl dymuniadau Schuster.

Pan ofynnodd Syr John Sankey, un o farnwyr yr Uchel Lys ar y pryd, am gael cyfarfod ag F.E. Smith, mynnodd Schuster fod Sankey yn cyfarfod ag ef, Schuster, hefyd.[25] Sicrhaodd ei fod ef yn derbyn copi o'r dystiolaeth yr oedd yr Arglwydd Ustus Bankes wedi ei rhoi i'r Is-bwyllgor yn ystod mis Chwefror.[26] Mae'n ddiddorol cofio mai Sankey a Bankes oedd dau o'r tri 'doethion' – y trydydd oedd yr Arglwydd Ustus Atkin – a luniodd Gyfansoddiad i'r Eglwys yng Nghymru yn ystod y cyfnod hwn,

[22] Llythyr (1/3/20) oddi wrth Syr Claud Schuster at Ei Anrhydedd y Barnwr R. Rowlands: "what it is beyond vague national sentiment which really actuates those who wish for a severance between Wales and England in these matters": National Archives, LCO 2/507.

[23] Llythyr oddi wrth Syr Claud Schuster at B.J. Bridgeman (4/3/20): National Archives, LCO 2/507.

[24] Llythyr oddi wrth y Barnwr R. Rowlands at Syr Claud Schuster (10/3/20): "National sentiment is no doubt largely responsible for the desire for *complete* severance between England and Wales – Many Welshmen demand for Wales the same position as that occupied by Scotland or Ireland. There are also practical objections to the present system": National Archives, LCO 2/507.

[25] Llythyr oddi wrth Syr Claud Schuster at Syr John Sankey (8/3/20): National Archives, LCO 2/507.

[26] Llythyr oddi wrth Syr Claud Schuster (9/3/20): National Archives, LCO 2/507.

cyfansoddiad a oedd yn cynnwys darpariaeth gynhwysfawr ar gyfer cyfundrefn o lysoedd i wasanaethu'r Eglwys ar ôl datgysylltu.

Ymateb Adran yr Arglwydd Ganghellor felly i'r cais am awdurdodaeth i Gymru oedd gwatwar y syniad fel un a oedd yn seiliedig ar 'deimladau cenedlaethol niwlog' a chasglu gwybodaeth er mwyn dangos bod y syniad yn un anfforddiadwy. Yn yr un modd ag yr oedd Edward Warton AS wedi gwatwar safon deallusion Cymru ddeugain mlynedd ynghynt, cwestiynodd Schuster a fyddai'n bosibl i Gymru gynhyrchu olyniaeth o wŷr talentog i fod yn fargyfreithwyr gerbron llysoedd Cymru ac i wasanaethu fel barnwyr ynddynt.[27] Awgrymodd y byddai'r cyfreithwyr mwyaf talentog yn parhau i symud i Lundain, ac na fuasai pobl llwyddiannus o'r fath yn fodlon symud yn ôl i weithio yng Nghymru.[28]

Ychydig sylw a gafodd unrhyw gysyniad cyfansoddiadol gan Adran yr Arglwydd Ganghellor, er gwaethaf eu barn cadarn nad oedd yn bosibl creu cyfundrefn farnwrol ar wahân ar gyfer tiriogaeth nad oedd yn meddu ar ei chyfreithiau ei hun. Dyna'r elfen wrth gwrs sydd wedi newid ers 1920. Yn y cyfamser dadbrofwyd y syniad bod y gwahaniaeth rhwng sefyllfa Cymru a sefyllfa'r Alban o ran eu cyfreithiau yn golygu nad yw'n bosibl i Gymru gael elfennau o awdurdodaeth ar wahân. Er nad oedd gan Gymru ei chyfundrefn farnwrol ei hun na chorff o'i chyfreithiau ei hun, fe gafodd Ysgrifennydd Gwladol ym 1964 a bellach wrth gwrs y mae gan y genedl y ddeddfwrfa Gymreig y dywedodd Cynhadledd y Llefarydd ym 1920 y dylai feddu ar yr hawl i ofyn am gyfundrefn farnwrol ar wahân hefyd.[29]

Er bod hynny'n wir, byddai'n ffôl credu bod y dadleuon a oedd yn seiliedig ar y gwahaniaethau hynny wedi llwyr ddiflannu. Maent naill ai yn parhau i fodoli neu wedi eu trawsnewid i ffitio'r sefyllfa newydd. Ym 1880, dadl Edward Warton AS oedd bod Cymru yn rhy fach i fod yn awdurdodaeth, bod ei chyfundrefn gyfreithiol yn un â Lloegr, nad oedd

[27] Memorandwm ymhlith papurau National Archives, LCO 2/507.

[28] Llythyr oddi wrth Syr Claud Schuster at Huw Edwards AS (26/4/20): "I do not think there is the smallest possibility that any Judge or Lord Justice who now holds office in the Supreme Court would abandon that office in order to have a place in a separate Welsh judiciary.": National Archives, LCO 2/507.

[29] "We recommend that any Devolution Statute should contain a clause providing in express terms that Wales may have a separate Judiciary and all needful accessory judicial institutions on application to the United Kingdom parliament by the Welsh Legislature.": National Archives, LCO 2/507, Draft Report, ¶ 22.

ganddi wŷr talentog a dim ond eithafwyr oedd yn dymuno gweld datblygiadau a oedd yn gwahanu'r ddwy genedl. Y mae'r union syniadau i'w gweld yn y dystiolaeth a gafwyd ac a gyhoeddwyd gan Bwyllgor Materion Cyfansoddiadol a Deddfwriaethol y Cynulliad eleni, er nad yw'r iaith mor ffyrnig.[30] Hyd yn oed mewn cylchgronau parchus fel yr *Economist*, wrth i'r cwestiwn o annibyniaeth ar gyfer yr Alban gael ei drafod yn gynharach eleni, fe gododd y bwgan mai teimladau cenedlaethol niwlog a oedd ar waith ac yn bygwth trechu egwyddorion ymarferol llawer mwy pwysig.[31]

Heb os nac oni bai, ac er gwaethaf y ffaith bod deddfwrfa bellach gan Gymru, ac o ganlyniad fod corff o gyfreithiau Cymreig yn datblygu, bydd gwrthwynebiadau cyllidol ac ymarferol Syr Claud Schuster yn parhau i gael eu defnyddio i wadu bod cyfundrefn farnwrol ar wahân yn bosibilrwydd o ddifrif. Ar ôl dweud hynny, mae yna wahaniaeth pwysig rhwng cyd-destun y ddadl ar ddechrau'r 20au â'r sefyllfa bresennol. Ym 1920, dim ond ar gyfer swyddogion y llywodraeth, y gweision sifil, yr oedd y manylion perthnasol ynglŷn â'r sefyllfa gyllidol ar gael; heddiw, yn rhinwedd datblygiadau fel y Ddeddf Rhyddid Gwybodaeth, mae o leiaf gyfle i gefnogwyr awdurdodaeth i Gymru feddu ar yr un wybodaeth os ydynt yn manteisio ar y cyfle.

---

[30] "There is a danger of throwing all this away to satisfy the insatiable demands of those who wish to have greater and greater devolution... There have always been only a few judges from Wales who were good enough for the High Court and Court of Appeal... There is just not the talent ... as Wales is a small country... a separate jurisdiction would mean the continuation of the downward slope to separation and the break-up of the UK." Gweler *Cynulliad Cenedlaethol Cymru: Y Pwyllgor Materion Cyfansoddiadol a Deddfwriaethol: Ymchwiliad i sefydlu awdurdodaeth ar wahân i Gymru – Ymatebion i'r ymgynghoriad* – Mawrth 2012: Tystiolaeth Dr. Peter Freeman, CLA WJ 1.

[31] "Some of the arguments for and against Scottish independence are aimed at the heart... If Scots really want independence for political or cultural reasons, they should go for it. National pride is impossible to price. But if they vote for independence they should do so in the knowledge that their country could end up as one of Europe's vulnerable, marginal economies. In the 18th century, Edinburgh's fine architecture and its Enlightenment role earned it the nickname "Athens of the North". It would be a shame if that name became apt again for less positive reasons." *The Economist*, 14–20 April 2012.

Cryfder y ddadl o blaid awdurdodaeth ar wahân i Gymru ar hyn o bryd yw'r ffaith y gellir bellach ei seilio ar egwyddorion cyfansoddiadol a chyfreithiol sydd wedi cael eu derbyn yn y gorffennol gan sefydliadau'r Deyrnas Unedig. Ffolineb felly, yn fy marn i, fyddai, ymadael â thir cadarn egwyddor er mwyn defnyddio dadleuon a all gael eu gwatwar fel teimladau niwlog neu eu gwrthwynebu ar sail cost neu ymarferoldeb. Dyma'r cwestiwn: a oes yna achos ar gyfer awdurdodaeth Gymreig, ac ni ddylai'r cwestiwn hwnnw gael ei ateb yn nhermau cyllid na phethau ymarferol, ond ar sail gyfansoddiadol. Mae gan Gymru gorff o gyfreithiau ac mae'n rhaid iddynt gael eu gweinyddu. Mae'r corff o gyfreithiau hwnnw bellach yn cynnwys cyfreithiau sydd yn cael eu gwneud gan ddeddfwrfa Gymreig a gweinidogion Cymreig sydd yn deddfu yn ddwyieithog. Felly, a ddylai llysoedd y tu allan i Gymru – lle nad yw cyfreithiau Cymreig yn gymwys, lle nad yw'r Gymraeg yn iaith swyddogol a lle nad oes hawl i ddefnyddio'r Gymraeg gerbron y llysoedd – a ddylai'r llysoedd hynny fod yn gymwys i weithredu cyfreithiau sydd yn gymwys yng Nghymru yn unig? Mae'n bwysig cofio mai yn 70au'r bedwaredd ganrif ar bymtheg y cafodd cyfundrefn farnwrol bresennol Cymru a Lloegr ei chreu er mwyn adlewyrchu'r gyfundrefn gyfreithiol oedd yn bodoli bryd hynny.[32] Pe bai cyfundrefnau barnwrol yn cael eu llunio heddiw ar gyfer Cymru a Lloegr, anodd credu y buasai'r penderfyniad o blaid un gyfundrefn ar gyfer y ddwy wlad, yn lle darpariaethau a fyddai'n adlewyrchu sefyllfa gyfreithiol bresennol y ddwy wlad. Ar ôl ateb y cwestiynau cyfansoddiadol hynny ar sail egwyddor y dylai cwestiynau cost ac ymarferoldeb gael eu hystyried, nid fel ffordd o ateb y cwestiynau cyfansoddiadol eu hunain. Mae'n bwysig bod cefnogwyr awdurdodaeth i Gymru yn sicrhau nad yw'r ddadl yn cael ei symud o dir cadarn y cwestiwn cyfansoddiadol at dywod symudol cyllid a phethau ymarferol.

Hefyd mae angen sicrhau nad yw'r egwyddorion cyfansoddiadol yn cael eu trawsnewid yn ystod y ddadl. Cymerwch ddadl aflwyddiannus Edward Warton AS ar ddechrau'r 1880au na ellid deddfu ar gyfer Cymru ar wahân i Loegr oherwydd nad oedd Cymru yn awdurdodaeth yn yr ystyr o fod yn diriogaeth â'i chyfundrefn farnwrol ei hun. Er bod Senedd y Deyrnas Unedig ers hynny wedi deddfu'n eithaf aml i Gymru ar wahân i Loegr, eto mae olion o'r ddadl yn parhau. Heddiw, y mae corff o gyfreithiau Cymreig

[32] Deddfau Barnweiniaeth 1873–75.

yn datblygu, cyfreithiau sydd yn gymwys yng Nghymru yn unig, ond, er gwaethaf hynny, y mae'r holl gyfreithiau hynny'n ymestyn neu'n rhychwantu dros Gymru a Lloegr. Paham? Oherwydd yn ôl yr athrawiaeth gyfreithiol a dderbynnir, mae'n rhaid i rychwant cyfreithiau gyd-fynd â ffiniau'r awdurdodaeth.[33]

Ystyriwch hefyd y ddadl a fynnodd nad oedd yn bosibl cael cyfundrefn farnwrol Gymreig heb fod corff o gyfreithiau Cymreig yn bodoli. Bellach, mae gennym gyfreithiau Cymreig, ond eto mae'r ddadl yn dal i gylchredeg, ond yn awr ar ffurf sydd wedi ei thrawsnewid, sy'n mynnu bod angen corff *digonol* o gyfreithiau. Mae'r datblygiad hwn ar y ddadl yn ddiddorol iawn, oherwydd nid yn unig y mae'r pyst yn cael eu symud, ond y mae natur sgorio gôl hefyd yn newid, oblegid mae'r cwestiwn "A oes gan Gymru ei chyfreithiau ei hun?" yn gallu cael ei ateb 'Oes' neu 'Nac Oes', ond gall yr ateb i'r cwestiwn "A oes gan Gymru ddigon o'i chyfreithiau ei hun i gyfiawnhau awdurdodaeth ar wahân?" amrywio yn ôl barn yr atebwr.

Wrth reswm, ni ellir dadlau o ddifrif bod nifer bach o gyfreithiau gwahanol yn cyfiawnhau creu cyfundrefn farnwrol ar wahân, ac mewn gwirionedd union yr un peth yw'r cwestiwn ynghylch digonedd nifer y cyfreithiau â'r cwestiwn sy'n gofyn a oes yna *gorff* o gyfreithiau yn bodoli. Eto, ar sail egwyddor, mae'n rhaid gofyn, pwy felly sydd yn meddu ar yr hawl i ateb y math hwnnw o gwestiwn a phenderfynu a oes yna ddigon o gyfreithiau Cymreig bellach i gyfiawnhau cyfundrefn farnwrol Gymreig? Yn ôl rhai o'r argymhellion a ystyriwyd gan Gynhadledd y Llefarydd ym 1920, deddfwrfa Gymreig a ddylai ateb y fath gwestiwn ac fe ddylai Senedd y Deyrnas Unedig dderbyn ei hateb a gweithredu i greu cyfundrefn farnwrol ar wahân.[34] Yn y pen draw, mater o egwyddor gyfansoddiadol sydd yma eto, sef cynrychiolwyr pobl Cymru a ddylai benderfynu'r

---

[33] Government of Wales Act 2006, Explanatory Notes, ¶¶ 333, 334b): "in order to be within the Assembly's legislative competence… the provision in question must apply only in relation to Wales"; ¶ 338b): "the provision in question may not "extend" to any jurisdiction other than England and Wales. (England and Wales is a single legal jurisdiction and Assembly Measures will form part of the law of that jurisdiction. Although they will only… apply to Wales". Gweler hefyd ¶¶ 404 a 405b) yn ail-adrodd yr athrawiaeth ynglŷn â Deddfau'r Cynulliad.

[34] "we think that the creation of a Welsh judiciary should be effected if and when the Welsh legislature shall ask for it.": National Archives, LCO 2/507, Draft Report, ¶ 22.

cwestiwn yn ôl eu barn hwy mewn modd sydd yn atebol i'r bobl a'u hetholasant.

Awgrymodd Cynhadledd y Llefarydd y dylai unrhyw ddeddf ddatganoli a fyddai'n creu deddfwrfa Gymreig gynnwys cymal yn datgan yn eglur y dylai Cymru gael ei chyfundrefn farnwrol ei hun unwaith y byddai deddfwrfa Gymreig yn gofyn amdani.[35] Yn anffodus, wrth gwrs, nid oes cymal o'r fath yn y statudau datganoli. Ond, unwaith eto, yr oedd y cysyniad o awdurdodaeth ar waith wrth i'r deddfau datganoli gael eu llunio, yn enwedig Deddf Llywodraeth(u) Cymru 2006. Yr ydym eisoes wedi nodi bod y gwahaniaeth rhwng *cymhwystra* a *rhychwant* cyfreithiau Cymreig yn deillio o'r syniad mai dim ond un awdurdodaeth sydd yn bodoli. Ond y mae'r cysyniad hyd yn oed wedi effeithio ar natur y setliad datganoli y mae Cymru'n meddu arno ar hyn o bryd. Yn ôl atodiad i'r dystiolaeth ysgrifenedig a gyflwynodd Ysgrifennydd Gwladol Cymru a Phrif Weinidog Cymru i Bwyllgor Dethol Materion Cymreig y Tŷ Cyffredin ym mis Tachwedd 2005, yr oedd yna ddau ddewis ynglŷn â sut i roi cymhwysedd deddfwriaethol sylfaenol i'r Cynulliad, sef:–

- penodi'r pynciau mewn perthynas â'r hyn y caiff y Cynulliad ddeddfu arno (y model penodedig); neu,
- rhoi cymhwysedd llawn i'r Cynulliad ddeddfu gan eithrio materion a neilltuwyd i Senedd y Deyrnas Unedig (y model neilltuedig, a ddefnyddiwyd ar gyfer cymhwysedd deddfwriaethol Senedd yr Alban).[36]

---

[35] "We recommend that any Devolution Statute should contain a clause providing in express terms that Wales may have a separate Judiciary and all needful accessory judicial institutions on application to the United Kingdom parliament by the Welsh Legislature.": National Archives, LCO 2/507, Draft Report, ¶ 22.

[36] *Primary Legislative Competence of the Assembly – Commentary*, tystiolaeth ysgrifenedig a gyflwynwyd gan Ysgrifennydd Gwladol Cymru a Phrif Weinidog Cymru i Bwyllgor Dethol Materion Cymreig y Tŷ Cyffredin, Atodiad 2, 10 Tachwedd 2005, ¶ 1:

> When defining the subjects on which the Assembly will be able, subject to a "yes" vote in a referendum, to exercise primary legislative powers there are two broad options:

Awgrymodd y dystiolaeth y cyntaf, a dyna'r opsiwn a ddewiswyd. Un o'r rhesymau dros y dewis oedd y ffaith nad oedd gan Gymru awdurdodaeth gyfreithiol ar wahân gyda chyfundrefn o lysoedd, barnwyr, proffesiwn cyfreithiol a darpariaeth ar gyfer addysg gyfreithiol. Yr oedd awdurdodaeth o'r fath yn cyd-fynd â'r gallu sydd gan Senedd yr Alban i wneud newidiadau ynglŷn â'r hyn a ddisgrifiwyd fel egwyddorion sylfaenol y gyfraith (*basic principles of law*).[37] Gan nad oedd gan Gymru awdurdodaeth gyfreithiol ar wahân, nid oedd yn addas i'w deddfwrfa feddu ar y gallu i wneud y fath newidiadau. Yn ôl yr atodiad, pe bai gan y Cynulliad yr un gallu cyffredinol i ddeddfu â Senedd yr Alban, buasai canlyniadau sylweddol ar gyfer undod awdurdodaeth gyfreithiol Cymru a Lloegr, oherwydd byddai'r llysoedd yn gorfod gweithredu egwyddorion a rheolau cyfreithiol yn gwbl wahanol mewn modd sylfaenol ar gyfer Cymru i'r rheini a weithredid ar gyfer Lloegr.[38] O ganlyniad, dewiswyd y model penodedig o ddatganoli pwerau deddfwriaethol.

> (a) to specify the subjects on which the Assembly may legislate (this is the model adopted in relation to Scotland in the Scotland Act 1978, which never came into force);
>
> (b) to provide that the Assembly may legislate on anything unless it is specifically reserved to the UK Parliament and then to specify those reserved matters (which is the model adopted in relation to Scotland by the Scotland Act 1998).

[37] Atodiad 2, n. 36 uchod, ¶ 3–4:

> Under the approach of the Scotland Act 1998 changes to the law which are made by the Scottish Parliament are not limited to specific subjects. They can include changes to basic principles of law.
>
> Scotland has its own distinct legal jurisdiction, with its own system of courts, judges, legal profession and provision for legal education. An ability on the part of its legislature to change basic principles of law and specific rules relating to subjects such as land law which have a general impact across almost all day-to-day activities is consistent with this situation.

[38] Atodiad 2, n. 36 uchod, ¶ 7:

Gadewch inni am eiliad ystyried rhesymeg yr atodiad. Ni ellir gwadu y byddai cymhwysedd deddfwriaethol ar y model neilltuedig yn rhoi'r gallu i'r Cynulliad newid egwyddorion cyfreithiol sylfaenol, ond posibiliad yn unig yw hynny; nid yw datblygiad o'r fath yn rhywbeth anochel. Os ydym yn edrych ar wledydd ledled y byd a oedd unwaith yn cael eu rheoli gan Brydain ond sydd bellach yn wledydd annibynnol gyda'u hawdurdodaethau cyfreithiol eu hunain, a ydym yn gweld gwahaniaethau o'r fath y mae'r atodiad yn eu hofni? Yr ateb clir yw 'Nac ydym'. Nid yn unig yng ngwledydd fel Awstralia a Chanada, sydd yn aelodau o'r Gymanwlad, ond hyd yn oed yng Ngweriniaeth Iwerddon a'r Unol Daleithiau, mae'r tebygrwydd rhwng y cyfundrefnau cyfreithiol yn parhau i fod mor agos ag i ganiatáu, er enghraifft, i athrawon cyfraith drosglwyddo heb lawer o drafferth o'r naill wlad i'r llall. Hefyd, ac yn bwysig iawn, mae gradd anrhydedd yn y cyfreithiau oddi wrth brifysgolion Cymru a Lloegr yn cael ei derbyn yn nifer o wledydd fel cymhwyster yn eu cyfraith hwy, ac mae nifer o wledydd yn parhau i fynnu bod eu bargyfreithwyr yn ymgymhwyso yng Nghymru a Lloegr. Cafodd Awstralia ei Senedd ei hun ar ddechrau'r ugeinfed ganrif, ond yr oedd yn dal yn bosibl anfon achos ar apêl terfynol at Bwyllgor Barnwrol y Cyfrin-Gyngor hyd at 1968, ac yr oedd y barnwyr a oedd yn eistedd ar achosion o Awstralia yn aml iawn i gyd yn tarddu o'r Deyrnas Unedig, heb unrhyw brofiad o ymarfer neu farnu yn Awstralia.[39]

> If the Assembly had the same general power to legislate as the Scottish Parliament then the consequences for the unity of the England and Wales legal jurisdiction would be considerable. The courts would, as time went by, be increasingly called upon to apply fundamentally different basic principles of law and rules of law of general application which were different in Wales from those which applied in England. The practical consequence would be the need for different systems of legal education, different sets of judges and lawyers and different courts. England and Wales would become separate legal jurisdictions.

[39] Gweler, fel enghraifft, *Overseas Tankship (U.K.) Ltd.* v *Morts Dock & Engineering Co. The Wagon Mound* [1961] AC 388, achos gerbron y Cyfrin-Gyngor o Awstralia gyda'r Arglwyddi Simonds, Reid, Morris o Borth-y-Gest, Radcliffe a Tucker fel barnwyr. Penderfynodd y Cyfrin-Gyngor argymell i'w Mawrhydi i ganiatau apêl y diffynnydd er bod Ustus Kinsella yn yr Uchel Lys ([1958] 1 Lloyd's Rep. 575) a thri barnwr apêl yn y Goruchel Lys ([1959] 2

Er y byddai'n bosibl i wahaniaethau difrifol ddatblygu yn egwyddorion sylfaenol y gyfraith, nid yw hynny wedi digwydd. Mae'n anodd credu, felly, fod yna berygl y byddai'r Cynulliad yn deddfu mewn modd mor wahanol ag i greu ymraniad llwyr â gwledydd eraill teulu'r Gyfraith Gyffredin.

Addysgiadol yw cofio, hefyd, bod barnwyr o'r Alban heb brofiad o ymarfer neu farnu yng Nghymru a Lloegr, ac er gwaethaf traddodiad cyfreithiol gwir wahanol eu mamwlad, nid yn unig y maent wedi cael eu derbyn fel rhai cymwys i eistedd ar achosion o Gymru a Lloegr yn Nhŷ'r Arglwyddi, bellach yng Ngoruchaf Lys y Deyrnas Unedig, ond wedi cael eu hystyried ymhlith barnwyr mwyaf disglair y Llys – ystyriwch, fel un enghraifft ragorol, yr Arglwydd Reid a'i gyfraniadau at ddatblygiad cyfraith Cymru a Lloegr mewn nifer o feysydd, yn aml iawn mewn partneriaeth â barnwr disglair arall, sef yr Arglwydd Morris o Borth-y-Gest. Yn yr un modd, y mae barnwyr o Gymru a Lloegr, heb unrhyw addysg neu brofiad yng nghyfraith yr Alban, yn eistedd yn rheolaidd fel barnwyr apêl terfynol ar achosion o Lys y Sesiwn yng Nghaeredin.[40] Os yw hynny'n bosibl ynglŷn â'r Alban, gyda hanes a thraddodiad cyfreithiol cwbl wahanol i Loegr, mae'n anodd credu na fydd barnwyr y Goruchaf Lys yn y dyfodol yn medru delio ag unrhyw ddatblygiadau a fydd yn deillio o gymhwyster deddfwriaethol y Cynulliad Cenedlaethol a dehongliadau llysoedd barn Cymreig.

Ni ellir beio gwleidyddion Cymru am gymryd yr hyn a oedd ar gael er mwyn datblygu hunaniaeth gyfreithiol y genedl, ond ni ellir chwaith osgoi'r ffaith bod gwleidyddion San Steffan ers talwm wedi cael y cysyniad o awdurdodaeth, gyda'i amryw ystyron, yn gyfleus iawn fel rheswm i wadu datblygiadau cyfreithiol i'n gwlad. Wrth bwysleisio bod angen cyfundrefn farnwrol ar wahân i gael cyfreithiau ar wahân, ceisiodd rhai rwystro deddfwriaeth ar wahân i Gymru, ac wedyn, pan ofynnwyd am gyfundrefn farnwrol, daeth yr ateb bod hyn yn amhosibl heb gyfreithiau gwahanol. Yn yr un modd, gwrthododd llywodraethau San Steffan am

---

Lloyd's Rep. 697) yn Ne Cymru Newydd wedi dyfarnu'n unfrydol o blaid y pleintydd.

[40] Gweler, fel enghraifft, *(M'Alister or) Donoghue* v *Stevenson* [1932] AC 562, lle buasai'r barnwyr o Gymru a Lloegr, yr Arglwyddi Buckmaster a Tomlin, wedi penderfynu yn erbyn barn y ddau farnwr o'r Alban, yr Arglwyddi Macmillan a Thankerton, oni bai bod yr Arglwydd Atkin wedi cefnogi barn yr Albanwyr.

ddegawdau ganiatáu Ysgrifennydd Gwladol i Gymru ar sail diffyg awdurdodaeth. Bellach, mae Ysgrifennydd Gwladol, deddfwrfa a llywodraeth ein hunain gennym, er bod cymhwysedd eang i ddeddfu wedi cael ei atal unwaith eto oherwydd diffyg… awdurdodaeth.

Eto, ymhlith y dadleuon dichellgar a ddefnyddiwyd yn ystod y ganrif a hanner ddiwethaf, y mae egwyddorion cyfansoddiadol clir i'w cael fel sail gadarn i ofyn am gyfundrefn farnwrol i Gymru. Bellach y mae gan Gymru gorff o'i chyfreithiau ei hun, corff sy'n mynd i ddatblygu a hynny drwy weithrediadau deddfwrfa a llywodraeth frodorol. Gan fod angen i'r cyfreithiau hynny gael eu gweinyddu, ac nad oes unrhyw reswm call am eu gweithredu y tu allan i Gymru, mae'r alwad am gyfundrefn farnwrol Gymreig yn ddadl gref ar sail egwyddor gyfansoddiadol sydd eisoes wedi cael ei chydnabod. Nid oes angen bellach wanhau'r ddadl drwy gymharu sefyllfa Cymru â sefyllfa'r Alban – a rhoi esgus i wrthwynebwyr chwilio am wahaniaethau rhwng y ddwy wlad, nac angen chwaith ddibynnu ar deimladau o genedlaetholdeb i gyfiawnhau'r alwad. Yn fwy pwysig byth, dylid osgoi gadael i'r gwrthwynebwyr symud y tir oddi wrth gwestiynau egwyddorol at gwestiynau cyllidol ac ymarferol. Ar ôl setlo'r egwyddor yw'r amser addas i ystyried y gost a phethau ymarferol. Mae hanes datblygiad cyfreithiol y Gymru gyfoes yn un diddorol iawn, ac y mae'r bennod olaf eto i'w hysgrifennu. Wrth i'r bennod honno gael ei hysgrifennu, byddai'n ddoeth cydnabod bod cynnwys y penodau cynharach nid yn unig yn ddiddorol ond hefyd yn addysgiadol.

Diolch yn fawr iawn.[41]

[41] Y mae'r awdur yn ddiolchgar iawn i'r Dr. Richard Crowe am ei sylwadau ar fersiynau Cymraeg a Saesneg y ddarlith hon.

DEVIOUS DEBATES AND DEVOLUTION

The History of the Campaign for a Welsh Jurisdiction

Thomas Glyn Watkin

LET me begin by thanking the Institute for Welsh Affairs for its kind invitation to me to deliver its annual lecture here at the Eisteddfod this year. It's an honour for me personally and also an opportunity to contribute to an important debate currently in the life of the nation.

A year ago, I had the privilege of contributing to a discussion on the Eisteddfod field in relation to a jurisdiction for Wales, a discussion that had been organized by the Law Society. In the meantime, the National Assembly has instituted an Inquiry by its Constitutional and Legislative Affairs Committee into the question,[1] and the Welsh Government has also launched a consultation on the same subject.[2] It was pleasing to behold the goodly number of responses received by the Constitutional Affairs Committee and to see how much interest there was now amongst the people of Wales in constitutional questions. It will be interesting to see what will result from all the work that is being done presently.

This is not, however, the first time that the question of a separate judicial system for Wales has been canvassed, and the concept of jurisdiction has been of importance in a number of debates concerning the legal status of Wales on more than one occasion. In the aftermath of the First World War, with the political map of Europe being redrawn, and even the political map of the British Isles being re-ordered as the Republic of Ireland left the United Kingdom, the question arose as to whether each part of what remained of the United Kingdom ought to have its own judicial system, that is separate jurisdictions for Northern Ireland, Scotland, and for England and Wales as distinct countries. During the deliberations of the Speaker's Conference, a Sub-Committee was established under Lord Stuart

---

[1] See *National Assembly for Wales: Constitutional and Legislative Affairs Committee: Inquiry into the establishment of a separate Welsh jurisdiction* – December 2011; *Consultation responses* – March 2012.

[2] See *Welsh Government: Consultation Document: A Separate Legal Jurisdiction for Wales* – Number WG-15109 (27 March 2012).

of Wortley to consider this specific question. At the end of the day, no conclusive answer to the question was forthcoming, but among the recommendations that were considered, the Committee suggested that the question of a separate judicial system for Wales was one that should be addressed by a Welsh legislature whenever such a body came into existence.[3] From the standpoint of 1920, this looks like a mighty kick into touch, but now, of course, the ball is back in play, and it's interesting to remember that the report in the 20s of the last century went on to say that any future devolution statute should contain a clause declaring clearly that the Westminster parliament should legislate to give Wales a judicial system whenever there was a request for such from a Welsh legislature.[4]

At the time, there was a lot of support for the idea of a separate judicial system for Wales amongst the country's lawyers, especially amongst the judiciary and the bar in south Wales.[5] It was also the case that some of the London-based officials of the British government argued strenuously against the idea, including Sir Claud Schuster, the Permanent Secretary at the Lord Chancellor's Office.[6] Schuster had been appointed to this post at a very young age, while still in his forties, and he was to stay in the post for over a quarter of a century. Consequently, he became very influential in his role as a civil servant, and more than once he used his influence to oppose legal developments regarding Wales. His argument in 1920 was that it wasn't possible for Wales to have a separate judicial system from England

---

[3] "the only competent judge of the strength and purpose of the Welsh desires for separate judicial arrangements from those of England would, in our opinion, be a Welsh legislature or other legislative authority specially constituted under a scheme of Devolution to represent the people of Wales": National Archives, LCO 2/507, Draft Report, ¶ 11.

[4] "we think that the creation of a Welsh judiciary should be effected if and when the Welsh legislature shall ask for it. It, if so desired, should be a Judiciary equal in independence to that of Scotland, with no appeal save to the House of Lords or its successor as the Supreme Appellate tribunal of the United Kingdom": National Archives, LCO 2/507, Draft Report, ¶ 22.

[5] Letter (24/2/20) from Sir Claud Schuster to His Honour Judge Rowland Rowlands: "I believe the scheme [for a separate Welsh judicial system] has a powerful backing": National Archives, LCO 2/507.

[6] See, Sir John Thomas, "Legal Wales: Its Modern Origins and its Role after Devolution – National Identity, the Welsh Language and Parochialism" in T.G. Watkin (ed.), *Legal Wales: Its Past, Its Future* (Cardiff, 2001), 113–166.

because Wales did not have its own laws. A separate body of law did not exist for Wales in the same way that a separate body of law existed in Scotland and in Northern Ireland. He employed the same argument almost a quarter of a century later when discussing with his fellow civil servants the question of a Secretary of State for Wales,[7] and one can to some extent discern Schuster's influence on the report in 1920 when one considers the connections between the case for a judicial system and the existence of a Welsh legislature, that is an institution with the power to create a separate body of law for Wales.

The argument is an interesting one, because it makes a clear connection between the concept of a jurisdiction and a body of law, but the argument is also surprising when one considers the legal history of Wales a generation earlier. For there was indeed a reason for the support shown by the judges and barristers of south Wales for the idea of a separate judicial system, a reason arising as a consequence of what had occurred forty years earlier when the Westminster parliament legislated for Wales separately from England for the first time. The statute in question was the Sunday Closing (Wales) Act 1881.

As the proposed legislation was debated before the House of Commons in 1880 and 1881, among its opponents was the Conservative member for Bridport, Edward Warton. On the basis of principle, his argument was that it was not possible to legislate for Wales separately from England because England and Wales were one – one integral territory served by one judicial system. Inasmuch as Wales did not have its own separate judicial system, it was not possible to legislate for it. Wales was not a jurisdiction, therefore it was not possible for it to have its own body of law.[8] The argument was

[7] Letter (18/5/44) from Sir Claud Schuster to Sir Alan Barlow: 'the Scottish and English judicial systems are, except for the appeal to the House of Lords, wholly distinct and separate, and operate a separate jurisprudence founded on different principles with different origins. The English and Welsh system of jurisprudence is a uniform integral whole operating a system of jurisprudence which is uniform, and has regard to the same principles, and springs from the same origins. The substantive law of England and Wales is not similar but the same, except for some minor immaterial differences.' National Archives, LCO 2/3214.

[8] Parl. Deb. (Series 3) vol. 253 (1880) HC 30 June: "were they to have fractional or national legislation? They all highly respected and loved Wales, but, after all, it was but a small part of England" (Edward Warton). "But he did not know that it

not successful – the Prime Minister himself, William Gladstone, went to the House in order to back the bill,[9] but it's clear that the argument made an impact upon the Welsh members and on the lawyers of Wales as they considered and remembered that Wales had its own law courts until 1830 – the Courts of Great Session – and if it was necessary for Wales to have its own judicial system in order to obtain its own enacted laws, perhaps it was time to get them back.[10]

Therefore, in the 1880s, the argument was that it was not possible for Wales to have its own laws because it didn't have its own law courts, and forty years later the answer to the request for Welsh law courts was that that was not possible because Wales did not have its own laws. Either there is an element of circularity in this argument, or – and very importantly in the context of the present discussions – it is not possible to have one without the other, that is – once more reflecting the recommendations of the 1920 report – a separate body of law calls for the existence of a separate judicial system.

Up to now, I have been avoiding using the term *jurisdiction* – and that for a reason. There is more than one meaning to the word, and that has enabled it to be used somewhat subtly from time to time in a manner which conceals the circularity of some of the arguments against the legal development of Wales. *Jurisdiction* can mean 'a territory which has its own laws'; it can also mean 'a territory which has its own judicial system'. As a consequence, one can say – as in the 1880s – Wales cannot have its own legislation because Wales is not a jurisdiction, and again, as in 1920, Wales cannot have its own judicial system because Wales is not a jurisdiction. The fact that the word can be used in more than one sense allows it to be used in a manner which is superficially consistent, but in truth the consistency is not merely superficial but false – and that has allowed it to be used in a pretty devious manner from time to time in order to justify withholding from Wales legal developments that were being permitted, for example, in relation to Scotland.

---

had been hitherto recognized that Wales should be treated in a different way from other portions of the Kingdom" (Arthur Peel).

[9] Parl. Deb. (Series 3) vol. 260 (1881) HC 4 May: cols. 1772–1775.

[10] "Wales should have restored to it the separate judiciary it once had": *Western Mail*, Friday, 26 March 1920.

Unfortunately, in the decades which followed, Scotland came to be used as a measuring rod virtually every time a question was raised regarding some distinct legal development for Wales. At the end of the 1930s, a little before the Second World War, the Government refused to let Wales have a Secretary of State of the same kind as Scotland possessed. Following a substantial increase in the special provision made for Scotland, the response of the Prime Minister, Neville Chamberlain, was that to compare Wales with Scotland was not relevant, because Scotland had its own legal system and administration even before the Scottish Office was created. Wales on the other hand had been incorporated into England during the sixteenth century without any law or administrative system which merited the attention of a special minister.[11] It is clear that comparing Wales with Scotland leads to unfavourable comparisons on the basis that Scotland was already a separate jurisdiction.

At the end of the Second World War, the whole body of Welsh MPs, with the support of some Welsh members of the House of Lords, asked that the question of a Secretary of State for Wales be reconsidered.[12] The Prime Minister, Winston Churchill, pleaded that the government was too busy with other matters to turn its attention to so complex an issue – an answer which is, in a way, perfectly fair given the country was emerging from a world war.[13] Despite that, however, one influential civil servant, Sir Alan

---

[11] Letter from Neville Chamberlain to Morgan Jones MP (27/7/1938): "The analogy of Scotland has been advanced … I think, however, that it must be recognised that the two cases are not parallel. For Scotland has always had different systems of law and administration from those in force in England… Wales, on the other hand, since Henry VII's (*sic*) Act of 1535, has been closely incorporated with England and there has not been, and is not now, any distinct law or administrative system calling for the attention of a separate Minister.": NLW, *James Griffiths Papers*, C2/1.

[12] Memorandum from all 36 MPs from Wales to the Prime Minister, Winston Churchill, (28/10/1943): National Archives, LCO 2/3214.

[13] Letter from Winston Churchill to Megan Lloyd George MP 2/1/1945: "Thank you for your letter of November 10 regarding the proposals of the Welsh Parliamentary Party for the establishment of a Secretary of State for Wales. The matter is, as you know, receiving consideration. The difficulty is that a proposal of this nature has such far reaching implications in the administrative sphere that detailed consideration has to be given it by the many authorities concerned. These

Barlow, found the time to write to Sir Claud Schuster at the Lord Chancellor's Office to draw his attention to the request.[14] His fear was that parity with Scotland would mean a separate judicial system, while noting that the law of Scotland, and not only its administration, was different from that which pertained in England, which was not the case with regard to Wales. In his reply, Schuster admitted that the Secretary of State for Scotland did not have many powers with regard to the administration of justice apart from appointing magistrates, but despite that fact he suggested that it would be wise to keep the question of a separate jurisdiction within view because there was in Wales a history of what he described as 'agitation' in relation to the subject.[15] Perhaps he was recalling the strength of feeling among the lawyers of south Wales after the First World War, but it is clear that he was unhappy with regard to what had been said by Ithel Davies in the 1930s to the effect that there would be a need to re-order the judicial system in Wales fundamentally if the Welsh language were to be accorded its proper place in the administration of justice in Wales,[16] words used before even the Welsh Courts Act was passed in 1942. It's perfectly clear this time that the civil servants were looking for reasons to refuse a legal development in relation to Wales, and that comparing Wales to Scotland gave them the opportunity to employ the subtle concept of jurisdiction as an excuse or a convenient reason for their refusal. There was a danger in comparing Wales to Scotland, and that danger continues to exist, and this is not the only sort of argument that it is dangerous to employ.

---

authorities are of course heavily burdened with war tasks.": NLW, *James Griffiths Papers*, C2/5.

[14] Letter from J.A. Barlow (Sir Alan Barlow) to Sir Claud Schuster (12/4/44): National Archives, LCO 2/3214.

[15] Memorandum from Sir Claud Schuster to Sir Alan Barlow (18/5/44) "It would, however, be unwise wholly to exclude from consideration the fact that there have been signs of agitation in Wales on this subject": National Archives, LCO 2/3214.

[16] In his memorandum (note 15 above), Schuster quoted from the evidence of Ithel Davies according to the Report of the Peel Commission (Cmd. 5065) 20/1/36, p. 371: "if the Welsh language is given its rightful and proper place in the administration of justice in Wales, there must be something like a fundamental reorganization of the judicial system in Wales to meet that measure of recognition": National Archives, LCO 2/3214.

The argument against separate legislation for Wales on the grounds that Wales did not have a separate judicial system and the argument that it was not possible to create a separate judicial system for Wales because Wales did not have its own laws, both – despite the circularity of their reasoning – were at least arguments on the basis of constitutional principle. However, it was not only on the basis of principle that opponents based their arguments.. From time to time, the idea of legal provision for Wales was mocked, perhaps to enrage its supporters and to provoke them to admit that nationalism was the principal foundation for their requests. In 1880 and 1881, Edward Warton MP argued hotly against specific legislation for Wales by stating that Wales was only a small part of England, although some people fancied that Wales was some sort of nation although it had never produced great men in the same way as Ireland.[17] At the end of the day, the intention of legislating for Wales separately from England was a sign of weakness in the eyes of Edward Warton, a weakness which amounted to giving in to the wishes of extremists – "the fads and fancies of fanatics".[18]

It is clear that there were very strong feelings at work on both sides of the debate during the 1880s. One cannot overestimate the contribution of Gladstone as Prime Minister in winning the day for the success of the bill. The principle of legislating separately for Wales was important to the Liberal Party and to Gladstone himself, for looking to the future the Act would be a foundation for the legislation that would disestablish the Church of England in Wales. That did not happen until shortly before the First World War, when a Welshman, David Lloyd George, was one of the foremost figures in the Liberal Party.

---

[17] Parl. Deb. (Series 3) vol. 253 (1880) HC., 4 May: "Why should they have one Sunday Closing Bill for Wales, whose population, after all, only formed a small section of the community, but who, following the example of the Irish, fancied themselves a nation, and quite as famous as Ireland, while in point of fact, the Principality was only a small part of England? Wales, certainly, had not produced great men like Ireland" (Edward Warton MP).

[18] Parl. Deb. (Series 3) vol. 253 (1880) HC., 15 June: "The great fallacy was in trying to set up different little laws all over England, breaking the United Kingdom into sections for the purpose of carrying out the fads and fancies of fanatics." (Edward Warton MP).

It was during Lloyd George's time as Prime Minister, of course, that the question of a separate jurisdiction for Wales fell to be considered as part of the work of the Speaker's Conference in 1920. By that time, Lloyd George was Prime Minister of a coalition government and the Lord Chancellor in his government was Lord Birkenhead, F.E. Smith, a former Conservative member of parliament and one of Lloyd George's fiercest opponents at the time of his truly revolutionary People's Budget in 1909, and also during the campaign to pass the legislation to disestablish the Church in Wales. As the Permanent Secretary of the government department which had F.E. Smith at the helm, Sir Claud Schuster decided to intervene in the work of the sub-committee of the Speaker's Conference that was, in 1920, considering a judicial system for Wales. It is difficult to believe that the strength of feeling exhibited by F.E. Smith during the debates on the Welsh Church Bill were not at work once more behind the scenes when Schuster wrote to the Speaker, James Lowther, in February 1920 to say that the Lord Chancellor wished to give evidence before the committee.[19] One must remember that this correspondence took place in the final weeks before the Welsh Church Act came into force at the end of March 1920.

Ten days after writing to the Speaker, Schuster wrote a letter to one of the County Court judges in south Wales, His Honour Judge Rowland Rowlands. In his letter, Schuster stated that he understood there to be a fair amount of support for the idea of a separate Welsh judicial system, while confessing that the idea was within limits desirable, but also expressing his concern that some of the proposals were too extreme, for instance, the notion of a separate Court of Appeal.[20] It would appear that Schuster was 'fishing' in his letter in order to find out the strength of the support for a separate jurisdiction for Wales together with the content of the proposals that the supporters would present to the Sub-committee. Judge Rowlands

---

[19] Letter from Sir Claud Schuster to James W. Lowther MP (13/2/20): National Archives, LCO 2/507.

[20] Letter (24/2/20) from Sir Claud Schuster to His Honour Judge Rowland Rowlands: "no doubt, within limits, the proposed change is desirable, but I have an idea that some of the proposals to be put forward – particularly those dealing with appeals etc. – are too extreme, at any rate for the present": National Archives, LCO 2/507.

answered straightforwardly with a comprehensive description of what a number of his fellow lawyers would like to see.[21]

Immediately he had received Rowlands' answer, the tone of Schuster's correspondence changed. He replied to Rowlands' letter by return, a reply bearing the date 1 March 1920, asking what it was that actuated such demands, other than 'vague national sentiment', and starting to argue that there was not sufficient business before the civil courts in Wales to justify such a development.[22] Without waiting for Rowlands to answer, he asked B.J. Bridgeman to undertake research into the costs of the County Courts in Wales and how much they raised in the way of fees.[23] It would appear that Schuster had deliberately contacted Rowlands in order to discover the strength and nature of the argument in favour of a jurisdiction for Wales in order to prepare the case against such a development for presentation before the Sub-Committee. The manner in which he wrote to Rowlands in February is so different from the manner in which he wrote on St. David's Day, after having received the information that he wanted, that it shows more than a trace of deviousness, particularly when one considers how swift was his uncompromising reply against the plan once he had the information in his hands. It's obvious too that Rowlands had appreciated the situation, for in his reply a week later, he denied that national sentiment alone was behind the campaign for a Welsh jurisdiction and set out a number of practical considerations which supported such a development.[24] Unfortunately, this moved the debate on to practical considerations, exactly what Schuster wanted.

---

[21] Letter from Judge R. Rowlands to Sir Claud Schuster (29/2/20): National Archives, LCO 2/507.

[22] Letter (1/3/20) from Sir Claud Schuster to His Honour Judge R. Rowlands: "what it is beyond vague national sentiment which really actuates those who wish for a severance between Wales and England in these matters": National Archives, LCO 2/507.

[23] Letter from Sir Claud Schuster to B.J. Bridgeman (4/3/20): National Archives, LCO 2/507.

[24] Letter from Judge R. Rowlands to Sir Claud Schuster (10/3/20): "National sentiment is no doubt largely responsible for the desire for *complete* severance between England and Wales – Many Welshmen demand for Wales the same position as that occupied by Scotland or Ireland. There are also practical objections to the present system": National Archives, LCO 2/507.

When Sir John Sankey, a High Court judge at that time, asked to meet with F.E. Smith, Schuster insisted that Sankey meet with him, Schuster, as well.[25] He ensured that he received a copy of the evidence that Lord Justice Bankes had given before the Sub-Committee during February.[26] It is interesting to note that Sankey and Bankes were two of the three 'wise men' – the third was Lord Justice Atkin – who drafted the Constitution of the Church in Wales at this time, a constitution which contained comprehensive provisions for a system of courts to serve the Church following disestablishment.

The response of the Lord Chancellor's department therefore to the request for a Welsh jurisdiction was to mock the idea as one based on 'vague national sentiment' and to gather information in order to demonstrate that the idea was unaffordable. In the same manner as Edward Warton MP had mocked the standards of Wales' intellectuals forty years earlier, Schuster questioned whether it would be possible for Wales to produce a succession of talented individuals to be barristers before the Welsh courts and to serve as judges in them.[27] He suggested that the most able lawyers would continue to move to London, and that successful people of the kind would not be willing to return to work in Wales.[28]

Little attention was paid by the Lord Chancellor's department to any constitutional concept, despite their firm belief that it was not possible to create a separate judicial system for a territory that did not possess its own laws. This is the factor, of course, which has changed since 1920, and in the meantime the idea that the difference between the position of Wales and that of Scotland as regards their laws means that it is not possible for Wales to have elements of a separate jurisdiction has been disproved. Despite the fact that Wales did not have its own judicial system nor its own body of laws, Wales got its own Secretary of State in 1964 and by now, of course,

---

[25] Letter from Sir Claud Schuster to Sir John Sankey (8/3/20): National Archives, LCO 2/507.

[26] Letter from Sir Claud Schuster (9/3/20): National Archives, LCO 2/507.

[27] Memorandum amongst the papers in National Archives, LCO 2/507.

[28] Letter from Sir Claud Schuster to Huw Edwards MP (26/4/20): "I do not think there is the smallest possibility that any Judge or Lord Justice who now holds office in the Supreme Court would abandon that office in order to have a place in a separate Welsh judiciary.": National Archives, LCO 2/507.

there exists a Welsh legislature, which the Speaker's Conference in 1920 said should have the right to ask for a separate judicial system as well.[29]

Albeit that that is the case, it would be foolish to believe that the arguments which were founded upon those distinctions have completely disappeared. They either continue to operate or have been adapted to fit the new situation. In 1880, Edward Warton MP's argument was that Wales was too small to be a jurisdiction, that its legal system was of a part with England, that it did not have individuals of talent and that only extremists wished to see developments that would divide the two nations. The same ideas can be seen at work amidst the evidence received and published by the Constitutional and Legislative Affairs Committee of the Assembly this year, albeit that the language is not quite as colourful.[30] Even in reputable journals such as the *Economist*, when the question of Scottish independence was discussed earlier this year, the spectre was raised that vague national sentiment was at work and threatening to defeat practical considerations of much greater importance.[31]

---

[29] "We recommend that any Devolution Statute should contain a clause providing in express terms that Wales may have a separate Judiciary and all needful accessory judicial institutions on application to the United Kingdom parliament by the Welsh Legislature.": National Archives, LCO 2/507, Draft Report, ¶ 22.

[30] "There is a danger of throwing all this away to satisfy the insatiable demands of those who wish to have greater and greater devolution… There have always been only a few judges from Wales who were good enough for the High Court and Court of Appeal… There is just not the talent … as Wales is a small country… a separate jurisdiction would mean the continuation of the downward slope to separation and the break-up of the UK." See *National Assembly for Wales: Constitutional and Legislative Affairs Committee: Inquiry into the establishment of a separate Welsh jurisdiction – Consultation responses* – March 2012: Evidence of Dr. Peter Freeman, CLA WJ 1.

[31] "Some of the arguments for and against Scottish independence are aimed at the heart... If Scots really want independence for political or cultural reasons, they should go for it. National pride is impossible to price. But if they vote for independence they should do so in the knowledge that their country could end up as one of Europe's vulnerable, marginal economies. In the 18th century, Edinburgh's fine architecture and its Enlightenment role earned it the nickname "Athens of the North". It would be a shame if that name became apt again for less positive reasons." *The Economist*, 14–20 April 2012.

Without a shadow of a doubt, and despite the fact that Wales now has its own legislature and that, as a consequence, a body of Welsh laws is developing, Sir Claud Schuster's financial and practical objections will continue to be called into play so as to deny that a separate judicial system is a serious possibility. Having said that, there is an important difference between the context of the debate in the 1920s and the present moment. In 1920, it was only the government officials, the civil servants, who had access to the relevant facts concerning the financial position; today, by virtue of developments such as the Freedom of Information Act, supporters of a Welsh jurisdiction at least have the opportunity to obtain the same information provided they take advantage of that opportunity.

The strength of the argument for a separate jurisdiction for Wales at the present time is that it can now be based on constitutional and legal principles that have been accepted in the past by the institutions of the United Kingdom. It would be folly therefore, in my opinion, to abandon the solid ground of principle in order to deploy arguments that are open to mockery as vague sentiment or opposition on the ground of cost or practicality. The question is whether there is a case for a Welsh jurisdiction, and that question ought not to be answered in terms of finance and practicality, but on a constitutional basis. Wales has a body of laws and those laws have to be administered. Further, that body of laws contains laws made by a Welsh legislature and by Welsh Ministers who legislate bilingually. Therefore, should courts outside of Wales, where the Welsh laws do not apply, where Welsh is not an official language and where there is no right to use the Welsh language before the courts, should such courts be competent to administer laws which apply only in Wales? It is important to remember that it was only in the 1870s that the current judicial system of England and Wales was created in order to reflect the legal system which existed at that time.[32] It is difficult to believe that if judicial systems were being designed today for England and Wales, the decision would be in favour of one system serving the two countries as opposed to provisions reflecting the current legal position of the two lands. It is after having answered that constitutional question on the basis of principle that the questions of cost and practicality should be considered, not to answer the constitutional questions themselves, and it is important that supporters of a

[32] Judicature Acts 1873–75.

jurisdiction for Wales ensure that the argument does not get moved from the firm ground of the constitutional question onto the shifting sands of costs and practicalities.

It is important also to ensure that the constitutional principles do not undergo adaptation during the course of the debate. Take Edward Warton MP's unsuccessful argument at the start of the 1880s that one cannot legislate for Wales separately from England because Wales is not a jurisdiction in the sense of being a territory with its own judicial system. Although Parliament has, since then, legislated quite frequently for Wales apart from England, yet vestiges of that argument remain. Today, a body of Welsh laws is developing, laws that apply only in Wales, but, despite that fact, all of those laws *extend* to England and Wales. Why? Because according to the accepted legal doctrine, the extent of laws has to correspond to the boundaries of the jurisdiction.[33]

Consider also the argument which insisted that it was not possible to have a Welsh judicial system in the absence of the existence of a body of Welsh laws. Nowadays, we have Welsh laws, but yet the argument is still advanced, but now adapted to saying that there must be a *sufficient* body of Welsh laws. This development of the argument is very interesting, because not only does it shift the goalposts, it also changes what is meant by scoring a goal, because the question "Has Wales got its own laws?" is susceptible to a 'Yes' or 'No' answer, but the answer to the question "Has Wales sufficient laws of its own to justify it having a separate jurisdiction?" can vary according to the opinion of the respondent.

To be reasonable, one cannot argue that a small number of distinct laws would justify the creation of a separate judicial system, and in truth the question of the sufficiency of the number of laws amounts to the same thing as asking whether a *body* of laws exists. Yet, as a matter of principle, one has to ask, who therefore has the right to answer that sort of question and to decide whether there is now a sufficient body of Welsh law to justify

---

[33] Government of Wales Act 2006, Explanatory Notes, ¶¶ 333, 334b): "in order to be within the Assembly's legislative competence… the provision in question must apply only in relation to Wales"; ¶ 338b): "the provision in question may not "extend" to any jurisdiction other than England and Wales. (England and Wales is a single legal jurisdiction and Assembly Measures will form part of the law of that jurisdiction. Although they will only… apply to Wales". See also ¶¶ 404 and 405b) repeating the doctrine in relation to Assembly Acts.

a Welsh judicial system. According to some of the recommendations considered by the Speaker's Conference in 1920, it was a Welsh legislature that should answer that sort of question and the United Kingdom parliament should accept its answer and act to create a separate judicial system.[34] At the end of the day, this is again a matter of constitutional principle, namely that it is the representatives of the people of Wales who should answer this question according to their view in a manner which is accountable to the people who elected them.

The Speaker's Conference suggested that any devolution statute establishing a Welsh legislature should contain a clause declaring clearly that Wales should have its own judicial system as soon as a Welsh legislature requested one.[35] Unfortunately, of course, there is no such clause in the devolution statutes. However, yet once more, the concept of jurisdiction was at work in the process of framing the devolution statutes, especially with regard to the Government of Wales Act 2006. We have already noted that the distinction between the *applicability* and the *extent* of Welsh laws arises from the idea that only one jurisdiction exists. However, the concept has affected even the kind of devolution settlement that Wales has obtained. According to an Appendix to the written evidence presented by the Secretary of State for Wales and the First Minister of Wales to the Welsh Affairs Select Committee of the House of Commons in November 2005, there were two options in relation to how to confer competence upon the Assembly to make primary legislation, namely:–

- to specify the subjects on which the Assembly may legislate (the conferred powers model); or,

- to provide that the Assembly may legislate on anything except matters reserved to the UK Parliament (the reserved

---

[34] "we think that the creation of a Welsh judiciary should be effected if and when the Welsh legislature shall ask for it.": National Archives, LCO 2/507, Draft Report, ¶ 22.

[35] "We recommend that any Devolution Statute should contain a clause providing in express terms that Wales may have a separate Judiciary and all needful accessory judicial institutions on application to the United Kingdom parliament by the Welsh Legislature.": National Archives, LCO 2/507, Draft Report, ¶ 22.

> powers model, used with regard to the legislative competence of the Scottish parliament).[36]

The evidence recommended the former, and that was the option chosen. One of the reasons for the choice was the fact that Wales did not have its own distinct legal jurisdiction, with its own system of courts, judges, legal profession and provision for legal education. A jurisdiction of that sort was consistent with the power of the Scottish parliament to make changes in relation to what was described as 'basic principles of law'.[37] As Wales did

---

[36] *Primary Legislative Competence of the Assembly – Commentary*, written evidence presented by the Secretary of State for Wales and the First Minister of Wales to the Welsh Affairs Committee of the House of Commons, Appendix 2, 10 November 2005, ¶ 1:

> When defining the subjects on which the Assembly will be able, subject to a "yes" vote in a referendum, to exercise primary legislative powers there are two broad options:
>
> > (a) to specify the subjects on which the Assembly may legislate (this is the model adopted in relation to Scotland in the Scotland Act 1978, which never came into force);
> >
> > (b) to provide that the Assembly may legislate on anything unless it is specifically reserved to the UK Parliament and then to specify those reserved matters (which is the model adopted in relation to Scotland by the Scotland Act 1998).

[37] Appendix 2, n. 36 above, ¶ 3–4:

> Under the approach of the Scotland Act 1998 changes to the law which are made by the Scottish Parliament are not limited to specific subjects. They can include changes to basic principles of law.
>
> Scotland has its own distinct legal jurisdiction, with its own system of courts, judges, legal profession and provision for legal education. An ability on the part of its legislature to change basic principles of law and specific rules relating to subjects such as land law which have a general impact across almost all day-to-day activities is consistent with this situation.

not have a separate legal jurisdiction, it was not appropriate for its legislature to have the competence to make such changes. According to the Appendix, 'if the Assembly had the same general power to legislate as the Scottish Parliament then the consequences for the unity of the England and Wales legal jurisdiction would be considerable', because 'the courts would, as time went by, be increasingly called upon to apply fundamentally different basic principles of law and rules of law of general application which were different in Wales from those which applied in England'.[38] As a result, the conferred powers model of devolving legislative competence was chosen.

Let us for a moment consider the reasoning of the Appendix. One cannot deny that the reserved powers model of devolving legislative competence would give the Assembly the power to change basic legal principles, but the use of that power is only a possibility; such a use is not inevitable. If we look at countries around the world that were once ruled by Britain but which are now independent and have their own legal jurisdictions, do we discover disparities of the kind which the Appendix fears? The clear answer is that we do not. Not only in countries such as Australia and Canada, which are members of the Commonwealth, but even in the Republic of Ireland and in the United States, the similarity between the legal systems continues to be close enough to permit, for example, law teachers to move without much difficulty from one country to another. In addition, and very importantly, an honours degree in law from universities in England and Wales is accepted in a number of countries as a qualification in their own law, and a number of countries continue to insist

---

[38] Appendix 2, n. 36 above, ¶ 7:

> If the Assembly had the same general power to legislate as the Scottish Parliament then the consequences for the unity of the England and Wales legal jurisdiction would be considerable. The courts would, as time went by, be increasingly called upon to apply fundamentally different basic principles of law and rules of law of general application which were different in Wales from those which applied in England. The practical consequence would be the need for different systems of legal education, different sets of judges and lawyers and different courts. England and Wales would become separate legal jurisdictions.

that their barristers qualify in England. Australia obtained its own parliament at the beginning of the twentieth century, but the possibility of sending a case on final appeal to the Judicial Committee of the Privy Council continued until 1968, and the judges who sat on cases from Australia very frequently were all from the United Kingdom, without any experience of having practised or having acted in a judicial capacity in Australia.[39] Despite the possibility that serious differences could develop in basic principles of law, that has not happened. It is difficult to believe, therefore, that there is a danger that the Assembly would legislate in so divergent a manner as to cause a total rift with other countries of the common law tradition.

It is instructive to remember, too, that judges from Scotland, without experience of practice or acting in a judicial capacity in England and Wales, and in spite of there being a really distinct legal tradition in their native land, were not only accepted as competent to sit on cases from England and Wales in the House of Lords, or now in the Supreme Court of the United Kingdom, but have been esteemed among the most distinguished judges of the Court – consider, one excellent example, Lord Reid and his contributions to the development of the law of England and Wales in a number of fields, often in partnership with another distinguished judge, namely Lord Morris of Borth-y-Gest. In the same way, judges from England and Wales, without any training or experience in the law of Scotland have regularly sat as judges of final appeal on cases from the Court of Session in Edinburgh.[40] If that is possible in relation to Scotland, with a legal history and legal tradition entirely distinct from that of

---

[39] See, for example, *Overseas Tankship (U.K.) Ltd.* v *Morts Dock & Engineering Co. The Wagon Mound* [1961] AC 388, a case before the Privy Council from Australia with Lords Simonds, Reid, Morris of Borth-y-Gest, Radcliffe and Tucker as judges. The Privy Council decided to recommend to Her Majesty that the defendant's appeal be allowed albeit that Kinsella J in the High Court ([1958] 1 Lloyd's Rep. 575) and three appeal judges in the Supreme Court ([1959] 2 Lloyd's Rep. 697) in New South Wales had decided unanimously in favour of the plaintiff.

[40] See, for example, *(M'Alister or) Donoghue* v *Stevenson* [1932] AC 562, where the judges from England and Wales, Lords Buckmaster and Tomlin, would have decided the case against the opinion of the two judges from Scotland, Lords Macmillan and Thankerton, were it not that Lord Atkin had supported the view of the Scottish judges.

England, it is hard to credit that in the future the judges of the Supreme Court could not cope with any developments which may arise from the legislative competence of the National Assembly and interpretation by Welsh courts.

One cannot blame Welsh politicians for taking what was on offer in order to advance the legal identity of the nation, but one cannot also escape the fact that politicians at Westminster have over a long period found the concept of jurisdiction, with its multiplicity of meanings, very convenient as a reason to deny legal developments to this country. By emphasizing that it was necessary to have a separate judicial system in order to have separate laws, some sought to block separate legislation for Wales, and then, when a judicial system was asked for, the answer came that this was not possible without separate laws. In the same manner, governments at Westminster refused for decades to allow Wales a Secretary of State on the basis that Wales lacked a jurisdiction. We now have a Secretary of State, and a legislature and government of our own, albeit that a broad competence to legislate has been withheld, once more because of the lack of… a jurisdiction.

Yet, amongst the devious arguments used during the last century and a half, there are clear constitutional principles to be discerned which can provide a firm foundation upon which to ask for a judicial system for Wales. Wales now has its own body of laws, a body which is going to develop, and that through the actions of a native legislature and government. As it is necessary for those laws to be administered, and there is no sound reason for them to be administered outside of Wales, the call for a Welsh judicial system has a strong argument based upon a constitutional principle which has already been established. There is no longer any need to weaken the argument by comparing the position of Wales to that of Scotland – and thereby provide opponents with an excuse to search for distinctions between the two countries, nor any longer any need to rely on national sentiment to justify the call. More important still, one should avoid allowing opponents to shift their ground from questions of principle to questions of finance and practicality. The appropriate time for considering questions of cost and practical issues is *after* having settled the question of principle. The history of the legal development of contemporary Wales is a very interesting one, and the final chapter has yet to be written. As that chapter is being written, it would be wise to acknowledge that the content of the earlier chapters is not only interesting but also instructive.

Thank you very much.[41]

[41] The authoir wishes to thank Dr. Richard Crowe for his comments on both the English and Welsh versions of this lecture.